basic
SPANISH
grammar

Other titles in this series:
Basic French Grammar by Valerie Worth-Stylianou   0 7195 7121 9
Basic German Grammar by John Clapham   0 7195 7122 7
Basic Italian Grammar by Tony Giovanazzi   0 7195 8501 5

© Richard Leathes 1996

First published 1996
by John Murray (Publishers) Ltd
50 Albemarle Street
London W1X 4BD

Layouts by D & J Hunter
Typeset by Servis Filmsetting Ltd, Manchester
Typeset in 11/12pt Galliard and 9/12pt Frutiger
Printed and bound in Great Britain by The University Press, Cambridge.

A CIP record for this book is available from the British Library.

ISBN 0 7195 7120 0

basic
SPANISH
grammar

Richard Leathes

JOHN MURRAY

CONTENTS

▼▼▼
INTRODUCTION

The aim of this book is to make the main points of Spanish grammar accessible and easy to remember for anyone wishing to learn or revise them. It takes a very straightforward approach and does not assume that you are already familiar with grammatical terms.

- The purpose of each rule and structure is clearly explained.
- Examples taken from everyday language show how each point is applied and help you to remember the way it works.
- Activities give opportunities to practise or revise each point; answers to the activities are provided.

Basic Spanish Grammar is ideal for independent revision or study, or to use alongside other course materials for reference and practice. It will be an invaluable help if you are in any of the following learning situations:

- working towards a language qualification or examination;
- taking a language component as part of a broader course such as business studies;
- brushing up on your Spanish in preparation for a holiday or business trip to a Spanish-speaking country;
- improving your grasp of Spanish for use at work.

▼▼▼

USEFUL POINTS OF INFORMATION

▼ Pronunciation and spelling in Spanish

▼ *The alphabet*

a	a	j	jota	r	erre
b	be	k	ka	s	ese
c	ce	l	ele	t	te
ch	che	ll	elle	u	u
d	de	m	eme	v	ve, uve
e	e	n	ene	w	ve doble
f	efe	ñ	eñe	x	equis
g	ge	o	o	y	i griega
h	hache	p	pe	z	zeta
i	i	q	cu		

Notice that there are three 'extra' letters in the Spanish alphabet. In traditional Spanish dictionaries **ch**, **ll** and **ñ** are treated separately and follow entries for **c**, **l** and **n** respectively. Thus, **chalet** will follow **cuyo**, **pollo** will follow **polvo** and **paño** will follow **pantufla**. Some modern dictionaries follow English practice.

As **b** and **v** are pronounced the same or virtually the same in many parts of the Spanish-speaking world, the two letters are often distinguished in the following way when spelling:

b: be de burro   *or*   be de Barcelona
v: ve de vaca   *or*   ve de Valencia
¿Cómo se escribe 'huevo'? Se escribe con ve de Valencia.
How do you spell 'huevo' (egg)? It is spelt with a v.

- **Consonants**
b & v At the beginning of a word and after **m** and **n** both are pronounced like an English *b*: **barco**, **valle**, **hambre**, **enviar**. Elsewhere they have a sound half way between an English *b* and *v* with the lips not quite meeting: **haber**, **vivo**, **calvo**, **alba**.

c   i) Before **a, o, u** or a consonant it is pronounced like the *c* in *cat*: **coche, cama, Cuba, acto**. If this *k* sound appears before **e** or **i**, **qu** must be used (see **q** below).
ii) Before **e, i** in northern and central Spain it is pronounced like the *th* in *thin* and in Andalucía and Latin America like the *s* in *soft*: **centro, ciudad**. Where this sound appears before **a, o, u** or a consonant, **z** is used (see below). In the combination **cc** the first **c** is hard and the second soft: **acción, lección**.

ch As in English: **chico, leche**.

d   i) At the beginning of a word and after **l** and **n** it is pronounced like an English *d*: **dar, aldea, andar**.
ii) Elsewhere the pronunciation tends towards that of the *th* in *this*: **nadar**, and in some regions it is not pronounced at all when it occurs at the end of a word or in the ending **-ado**: **cuidado, Madrid, usted**.

f   As in English. The combination **ph** does not exist in Spanish: **foto, elefante**.

g   i) Before **e, i** it is pronounced like an English *h*, though a little stronger: **girar, gente**.
ii) Before **a, o, u** or a consonant it is a weaker version of the *g* in *garden*: **ganar, gordo, gusto, gloria**. U is not pronounced when it appears between **g** and **e** or **i**, but changes the sound of the **g** from that in (i) to that in (ii): **guía, guerra, distinguido**. To pronounce the **u** in this position, a diaeresis must be placed over it: **vergüenza, pingüino**.

h   Always silent in Spanish: **hombre, hijo**.

j   Pronounced like **g** (i) and appears chiefly before **a, o, u**: **jarra, joven, jugo**. The main exceptions to this rule are words derived from other Spanish words written with a **j**: **rojo – rojizo, dejar – dejé**; words beginning with **eje-**: **ejemplo**; or ending in **-je, -jero, -jería**: **viaje, viajero, cerrajería**, *but not* **auge, cónyuge**; and the preterite of verbs with no hard *h* sound in their infinitive: **traer – traje, decir – dije**, etc. The **j** at the end of a word is often not pronounced in everyday speech: **reloj**.

k   As in English. Only used in loan words: **kilo**, etc. Otherwise the sound is rendered by **c** or **qu**.

l	As in English.
ll	In northern and central Spain it is pronounced like the *li* in *million*, in Andalucía and Latin America like a *y*, and in a few parts of South America, chiefly the River Plate region, like the *s* in *measure*: **llave, calle**. An unstressed **i** never follows **ll** in Spanish: **millón**, *but* **bullía**.
m	As in English.
n	As in English.
ñ	Pronounced like the *ni* in *onion*. As with **ll**, it is never followed by an unstressed **i**: **riñendo**, *but* **reñía**.
p	As in English.
q	As in English. The **u** following is always silent: **que, quince**. This is the normal representation of the *k* sound before **e, i**. Elsewhere **c** is used, as in representing the *kw* sound: **cuestión, cuando**, etc.
r	Rolled, similar to Scottish practice: **señor**. Pronounced like **rr** at the beginning of a word: **rápido**.
s	As in *same*: **casa, salir**. *Except* before **b, d, g, l, m, n**, when it is pronounced like an English *z* or the *s* in *rose*: **resbalar, desde, rasgo, asno, mismo**. In some regions, mainly in parts of Latin America, it is pronounced like a Spanish **j** before a hard consonant: **este, España**.
t	As in English.
v	See under **b**.
w	It only exists in loan words and is generally pronounced as in English: **water, whisky, weekend**. Sometimes it is rewritten as a **v** and pronounced accordingly: **vagón, vals**.
x	Generally pronounced as in English: **éxito, examen**. Many pronounce **x** before a consonant or at the end of a word as the **s** in **casa**: **texto, fax**.
y	In most parts of Spain and Latin America it is pronounced as in English.

The unstressed **i** sound is written as **y**:

- at the beginning of a word, or after a prefix: **yo, cónyuge**
- between two vowels: **cayó, maya** (*but* **caía**) (In these two cases it is pronounced like *s* in *measure* in the River Plate region.)

- at the end of a word: **rey, buey, soy** (*but* **leí**).
- in the word **y** (*and*), which is pronounced the same as the Spanish **i**.

z   The same pronunciation as **c** (ii). It occurs before **a, o, u**, consonants, and at the end of a word: **zapato, zorro, azufre, luz**. *Exceptions*: a few words of foreign derivation.

The main spelling changes noted above may be summarised as follows:

English sound:		*k*	*th*	*hard g*	*hard h*	*gw*
Spanish spelling	before **a, o, u** or consonant at end of word	c	z	g	j	gu
	before **e, i**	qu	c	gu	g(j)	gü

Examples:

conocer – conozco	pago – pagué
vez – veces	coger – cojo
rico – riquísimo	averiguo – averigüé

- **Vowels**

a   Similar to *u* in *butter* in southern England: **bata, padre**.
e   A little sharper than the *e* in *set*: **este**.
i   Similar to the *ee* in *meet*: **hijo**
o   Similar to the *o* in *often*: **hombre**.
u   Similar to the *oo* in *food*, but shorter: **luna**.
       See also notes on **g** and **q** above.

- **Diphthongs** (pairs of vowels)

ai/ay   Similar to the *i* in *ride*: **baile, Paraguay**.
au   Similar to the *ou* in *round*: **causa**.
ei/ey   Similar to the *ay* in *hay*: **peine, rey**.
eu   Combination of the **e** and **u** sounds described above joined together (no English equivalent): **deuda**.
ie*   Similar to the *ye* in *yet*: **cien**.
ua*   Similar to the *wo* in *won*: **cuatro**.
ue*   Similar to the *we* in *wet*: **jueves**.
uo*   Similar to the *wa* in *water*: **cuota**.

* If these sounds occur at the beginning of a word they are always preceded by **h**: **hielo, huaso, huevo**. In the first case some words are written **ye-**: **yeso**.

- **Double letters**
These are only used in Spanish if they produce a sound different from that of the two single letters (**cc, ll, rr** above), or are pronounced separately, as in the case of **ee: leer, cree,** or **oo: sentándoos.** The combination **nn** occurs in words beginning with **n** preceded by a prefix ending in **n**, the commonest of these being **con-, en-, in-: connotación, ennegrecer, innecesario.**

- **Capital letters**
Unlike English, these are not used in Spanish for:

the word *I* (**yo**)

days of the week and months of the year:

sábado   *Saturday*   enero   *January*

any adjectives, even if these are used as nouns:

los ingleses   *the English*
los países católicos   *Catholic countries*

unless forming part of a name:

las Naciones Unidas   *the United Nations*

titles, except Saints:

el cardenal Cisneros, el duque de Alba, don Gumersindo, el señor Sanz

but:

San Pablo   *Saint Paul*

(They are optional with royal titles and Popes.)

As in English, capital letters are used at the beginning of a sentence and for abbreviations:

Lunes, el dos de agosto ...   Sr. D. Enrique Muñoz, etc.

In the case of titles of books, films, etc., only the first word is written with a capital letter unless names of people, places, etc. are involved:

La guerra de las galaxias   *Star Wars*

but:

La casa de Bernarda Alba   *The House of Bernarda Alba*

The acute accent is normally omitted from capital letters:

MALAGA *for Málaga*

▼ Accents – how and why they are used

The following three accents are used in modern Spanish: ¨ ~ ´

- ¨ is only used with **u** – see under **g** on page 2.
- ~ is only used with **n** – see under **ñ** on page 3.
- ´ can be used with any vowel, **a, e, i, o** or **u**.

▼ *Use of the acute accent (´)*

- **To show irregular stress**

The normal rules for stress are as follows:

Words ending in a vowel, **n** or **s** are stressed on the last syllable but one: **ca**sa, **li**bro, **jo**ven, **lu**nes.

Words ending in a consonant other than **n** or **s** (and including **y**) are stressed on the last syllable: co**mer**, pa**pel**, ver**dad**, es**toy**.

Wherever these rules are broken an accent is placed over the stressed vowel. Examples:

café, camión, ananás
árbol, lápiz, mártir, vivió, cuídate, sábado, exámenes

- **To show where the stress falls when two or three vowels are grouped together but should be *pronounced* separately.** Examples:

oído, veníais

This applies even when the vowels are separated by **h**: prohíbe.

- **To distinguish between two words of different meaning or function otherwise spelt the same**

The accent is placed on the vowel which carries the stress. These fall into three groups:

unaccented		accented	
adjectives		*pronouns*	
mi	*my*	mí	*me*
tu	*your*	tú	*you*
el	*the*	él	*he*

demonstrative adjectives		demonstrative pronouns	
este	*this*	éste	*this one*
ese	*that*	ése	*that one*
etc.		etc.	

relative pronouns, etc.		interrogative and exclamatory pronouns, etc.	
que	*who, which*	¿qué? ¡qué!	*who? which? what a!*
quien	*who*	¿quién?	*who?*
donde	*where*	¿dónde?	*where?*
adonde	*where . . . to*	¿adónde?	*where . . . to?*
cuando	*when*	¿cuándo?	*when?*
cual	*which*	¿cuál?	*which?*
cuanto	*as much as*	¿cuánto? ¡cuánto!	*how much? how!*

The accents are used in both direct and reported questions and exclamations:

¿Dónde está la leche?	*Where's the milk?*
Preguntó dónde estaba la leche.	*He asked where the milk was.*
¡Cuánto lo siento!	*How sorry I am!*
Dijo cuánto lo sentía.	*He said how sorry he was.*

miscellaneous

aun	*even*	aún	*still, yet*
como	*as, like*	cómo	*how*
de	*of, from*	*dé	*give*
mas	*but*	más	*more*
se	*(3rd person reflexive pronoun)*	sé	*I know*
si	*if*	sí	*yes, (him)self, etc. (reflexive pronoun after preposition)*
solo	*alone*	sólo	*only*

*The accent is removed when a single object pronoun is added to it: **deme**, etc.

▼ *Accents in compound words*

In compound words the first part loses any accent it had originally: **décimo + séptimo – decimoséptimo, río + platense – rioplatense**

except in the case of: adverbs ending in -**mente**: fácilmente
hyphenated words: soviético–japonés

▼ Punctuation in Spanish

▼ *The main ways in which Spanish differs from English*

- Inverted question marks and exclamation marks are used at the beginning of a question or exclamation as well as upright ones at the end. They may be found at the beginning or in the middle of a sentence and are used with the upright ones to separate the relevant phrase (see below).

- A dash is used at the start of dialogue. It is always used as the first part of the English inverted commas, but only as the second part when followed by an expression of saying, replying, etc.:

–Eres español ¿no? – preguntó.	*'You're Spanish, aren't you?' he asked.*
–Sí.	*'Yes.'*
–¿Dónde vives?	*'Where do you live?'*
–En un pueblo que se llama Cuacos en la provincia de Cáceres.	*'In a village called Cuacos in the province of Cáceres.'*
–¡No me digas! Lo conozco bien – siguió. – Mi hermana vive allí.	*'Well, I never! I know it well,' he continued. 'My sister lives there.'*

- After the greeting in a letter put a colon:

Muy señor mío: *Dear Sir,*   Querida Rosa: *Dear Rosa,*

▼ *Punctuation used in large numbers and decimals*
This table summarises the differences:

English:	2,500,000	1995	1.5%
Spain:	2.500.000	1.995*	1,5%
Latin America:	2,500,000	1,995*	1.5%

*The full stop or comma may be used with dates as well.

▼ Titles and forms of address

▼ *The Spanish words for you*
informal: **tú** (singular), **vosotros** (masc. plural), **vosotras** (fem. plural).

formal: **usted, Vd.** (singular), **ustedes, Vds.** (plural).

Tú and **vosotros** are used when addressing members of the family, friends, young people, and animals. At other times, **usted** and **ustedes** are used. Each has a corresponding set of object pronouns and possessives. **Vd.** and **Vds.** take the third person forms throughout (see pages 27–9, 36, 37, 45):

Usted **es** inglés.	*You are English.*
su casa y la mía	*your house and mine*
Les llamaré mañana.	*I will call you tomorrow.*

In Latin America **vosotros** is never used for you plural, only **ustedes**. The distinction between **tú** and **usted** is still maintained in the singular.

▼ *Mr, Mrs, Miss*
The Spanish equivalents are: **Señor** (**Sr.**), **Señora** (**Sra.**) and **Señorita** (**Srta.**)

Many people in the Spanish-speaking world use two surnames. In the case of men and the maiden name of women, the first surname is that handed down by the father, the second that handed down by the mother:

Rafael **Arce**=Cristina **Paz**

Ana **Ulloa**=Luis **Arce Paz**   Rosa **Arce Paz**=José **Villa**

Isabel **Arce Ulloa**   Gustavo **Villa Arce**

The first surname is the more important and the one normally used if either is to be used in isolation, as in conversation, or the one the person will be listed under in a telephone directory, etc.

Married women may choose to be addressed by their maiden name, or they may take on their husband's first surname in place of their mother's maiden name and preceded by **de**. Thus the women above would be called in full:

Sra. Ana Ulloa de Arce; Sra. Rosa Arce de Villa

Don, Doña is an informal title of respect given to people in authority or of some standing in society. It must always be used with a Christian name:

don Alejandro Cambó; doña Cristina Quiroga;
¡Buenas tardes, don Alejandro!

▼▼▼
NOUNS & ARTICLES
names of people, places and things

Nouns are words used to refer to any sort of 'things', from objects (*book, moon*) to abstract states or qualities (*happiness, freedom*) to names (*Madrid, Peter*).

▼ Masculine and feminine nouns

All nouns in Spanish are either masculine or feminine. Sometimes a noun's gender is obvious: **rey** (*king*) is masculine and **madre** (*mother*) is feminine. But usually you have to learn the gender of each new noun you come across.

■ **Feminine nouns**

Female people, animals, etc.: **la madre, tía, reina, vaca.**

Letters of the alphabet: **la be mayúscula, la ese minúscula** (*capital B, small s*)

Names of islands: **Mallorca es bella.**

Countries, regions, continents, and generally towns, etc. ending in unstressed a: **Francia, Europa, Galicia.**

Nouns ending in:

	main exceptions
-a	**el día, mapa, planeta** and most nouns ending in -ma: **el tema, problema,** etc.
-ción, -sión and most other nouns ending in -ión	**el avión, camión**
-dad, -tad, -tud	
-dez	
-ed	**el césped**
-ie	**el pie**
-itis	
-iz	**el lápiz, el tapiz**
-sis	**el análisis, el énfasis, el paréntesis**
-umbre	

■ Masculine nouns

Male people, animals, etc.: **el padre, príncipe, toro**

Days of the week, months, years, numbers.

Mountains (except where **montaña** or **sierra** are used), seas, deserts, winds, volcanoes, points of the compass, and usually rivers: **el Sahara, el Caribe, el Sur, el Amazonas.**

Countries, regions, continents, and generally towns, etc. not ending in unstressed **a**: **el Canadá, el Ártico, El Ferrol.**

Trees, except **la haya** (*beech*), **la higuera** (*fig tree*), **la palmera** (*palm tree*).

Other parts of speech used as nouns: **el sí, el adiós, un no sé qué,** etc.

Most compound nouns (nouns made by combining two or more words): **el paraguas, el pasatiempo, el altavoz.**

Nouns ending in:

	main exceptions
-o	**la mano, foto**(grafía), **moto**(cicleta)
-e (most)	**la ave*, calle, carne, clase, corte, fe, fiebre, frase, fuente, gente, hambre*, leche, llave, muerte, nave, nieve, noche, nube, parte, sangre, suerte, tarde, torre**
-i	**la bici**(cleta), **metrópoli**
-l	**la cal, cárcel, catedral, miel, piel, sal, señal**
-r	**la coliflor, flor, labor**
-u	**la tribu**
-y	**la ley**

*See page 13.

Some nouns can be either masculine or feminine without any change in ending. Any accompanying articles, adjectives, etc. agree with the person in question: **el/la turista, dentista, joven, estudiante, médico, colega,** etc.

The following are always feminine, even when the person they refer to is male: **estrella** (*star*), **persona, víctima, visita**

▼ Plurals

- Nouns ending in an unstressed vowel add -s: **vaca** – **vacas**.

Those ending in a consonant or stressed vowel add -es: **flor** – **flores, ciudad** – **ciudades, rubí** – **rubíes**.

Exceptions:

café, canapé, mamá, papá, pie, sofá, té add -s only; likewise some words of foreign origin and ending in a consonant: **coñacs, clubs, jerseys**, etc.

Words with a final unstressed syllable ending in -s do not change in the plural: **los lunes, las dosis, los paraguas,** *but:* **el dios** – **los dioses, el marqués** – **los marqueses**.

Although a written accent may need to be added or removed when making a noun plural, the spoken stress does not change. The only two exceptions to this rule are **carácter** and **régimen** which become **caracteres** and **regímenes** in the plural.

Surnames are generally left unchanged in the plural, but they can add a plural ending, unless they end in -z or -s or are composed of more than one name: **los Quintero(s)** *but* **los Ramírez, los García Pelayo**.

Remember the spelling and accent rules (pages 1–6) when forming the plural, e.g.:

la voz	las voces	el autobús	los autobuses
el joven	los jóvenes	la canción	las canciones

- Masculine plural nouns are used to describe mixed groups of both sexes: los padres (*parents*), hijos (*children, sons and daughters*), hermanos (*brothers and sisters*), reyes (*the king and queen*), etc.

- Some nouns may be used both in the singular and plural in Spanish but not in English:

el mueble	*piece of furniture*	los muebles	*furniture*
la noticia	*item of news*	las noticias	*the news in general*
el negocio	*a business or transaction*	los negocios	*business in general*

- Some nouns are plural in English but singular in Spanish when referring to only one unit or collective group, for example:

la Edad Media	the Middle Ages	el billar	billiards
la ropa	clothes	el pijama	pyjamas
la aduana	customs (e.g. at frontier)	el bosque	woods

and words ending in -*ics* (the Spanish equivalent normally being -**ica**):

la física	physics	la política	politics
but: el atletismo	athletics		

- English often uses a plural in the following type of situation, but Spanish uses the singular instead:

Levantaron la cabeza.	They raised their heads. (literally: They raised the head – they only have one head each)

▼ Activity 1 — *Plural nouns*

Put the nouns in brackets into the correct plural form:

Delante de la estación hay unas (flor) y unos (árbol); detrás hay dos (tren) y varios (vagón). En la calle hay muchos (coche), cuatro (taxi) y tres (autobús). A la derecha hay un almacén que vende (sofá), (silla) y (sillón).

▼ Articles

▼ Definite article (the)

There are four different words which mean *the*. The one to use in each case depends on the noun which follows:

	singular	plural
masculine:	el	los
feminine:	la	las

Note: **El** is used instead of **la** when it comes directly before a feminine singular noun beginning with a stressed **a** or **ha**:

el agua	*but*	**la** mejor agua	**la** acción
el haba	*but*	**la** mejor haba (article not directly before noun)	**la** hormiga (stress not on first syllable)

This makes the words easier to pronounce. They are still feminine and the plural is not affected: **las** aguas, **las** habas.

When **a** (*to*) and **de** (*of, from*) are followed by **el**, they join with it to become **al** and **del**:

Escribo **al** médico.	*I'm writing to the doctor.*
la casa **del** amigo	*the house of the friend, the friend's house*

but:

Llamo **a los** estudiantes.	*I call the students.*
la luz **de la** luna	*the light of the moon, the moonlight*

An exception is often made when **el** forms part of a name:

el monasterio **de El** Escorial	*the monastery of El Escorial*
con respecto **a El** Salvador	*with regard to El Salvador*

▼ *Where the definite article is used in Spanish but not in English*

• Before nouns used in a general sense:

la vida y **la** muerte	*life and death*
La gasolina es cara.	*Petrol is expensive.*

except in a few special cases:

Ella es fuerte en historia.	*She is good at history.*
a decir verdad	*to tell the truth*

• Before names of languages:

Habla bien **el** árabe.	*She speaks Arabic well.*
El ruso es difícil.	*Russian is difficult.*

except after **en**, or **de** introducing an adjectival (descriptive) phrase:

en alemán	*in German*
Es profesor de portugués.	*He is a teacher of Portuguese.*

It is usually omitted immediately after **hablar** and a few other common verbs:

Habla sueco.	*He speaks Swedish.*
Sabe (el) holandés.	*She knows Dutch.*
Estudian (el) griego.	*They are studying Greek.*

- Before names with titles or accompanied by an adjective:

La señora de Ortega vive aquí.	*Sra. Ortega lives here.*
la pobre Begoña	*poor Begoña*
el rey Carlos III	*King Charles III*

except:

with **San/Santo(a)**, **don/doña**, **fray**, **sor**, and foreign titles:

San Pedro, doña Inés, Míster Jones

when the person is being addressed directly:

Buenos días, Señorita Urrutia	*Good morning, Srta. Urrutia*

- Before certain place names:

los Países Bajos (*the Netherlands*), el Líbano, El Salvador, el Vaticano, el Reino Unido (*United Kingdom*)

and countries preceded by **Unión** or **República**:

la Unión Europea, la República Dominicana

- Before seasons, except after **en** or **de**:

No le gusta **el** invierno.	*He does not like the winter.*

but:

En verano irán a California.	*In the summer they are going to California.*
ropa de verano	*summer clothing*

- Before academic, religious and official buildings, meals, games, and some other nouns:

en la iglesia	*in church*	el desayuno	*breakfast*
en la universidad	*at university*	Juega al	*She plays basketball.*
a la escuela	*to school*	baloncesto.	
en el hospital	*in hospital*	en la cama	*in bed*
a la cárcel	*to prison*	en el trabajo	*at work*
pasar por la aduana	*to go through customs*	en la cuidad	*in town*
		en el mar	*at sea*
en el tribunal	*at court*	en la Tierra	*on Earth*

but note: ¿Dónde está correos?　　*Where's the post office?*

- When the verb **tener** is used with a part of the body or a piece of clothing accompanied by an adjective:

Tiene la nariz grande.
Tenías la camisa muy sucia.
(See also pages 27–8)

He has a large nose.
Your shirt was very dirty.

See also Percentages (page 138), Time (page 139), Age (page 143).

▼ *Where the definite article is used in English but not in Spanish*

- In some set expressions, for example:

por primera vez	*for the first time*
en primer lugar	*in the first place*
a principios de	*at the beginning of*
en medio de	*in the middle of*
a orillas de	*on the shores of*

- In the following type of royal title:

Jorge sexto

George the Sixth

▼ *Indefinite article (a, an, some)*

Like the definite articles, the indefinite articles in Spanish always agree with the nouns which follow:

	singular *(a, an)*	**plural** *(some)*
masculine:	un	unos
feminine:	una	unas

▼ *Where the indefinite article is used in Spanish but not in English*

Normally before an abstract noun accompanied by an adjective:

Tiene **una** habilidad sorprendente.

She has surprising ability.

▼ *Where the indefinite article is used in English but not in Spanish*

- Before a noun showing geographical origin, rank, occupation, religion, politics when used after **ser** and similar verbs:

Es capitán	*He is a captain*
Se hizo abogado.	*He became a lawyer.*

except where it is individualised or where there is also an adjective:

Es **un** futbolista famoso.	*He is a famous football player.*

- Before **cierto, ciento, medio, mil, otro, semejante, tal**, or with **que**:

cierta mujer	*a certain woman*
medio kilo	*half a kilo*
tal edificio	*such a building*
¡Qué blusa tan bonita!	*What a pretty blouse!*

Un tal exists with the meaning *a certain*: **un tal** Sr. Balmes.

- After expressions translating *as* or *for* (in the manner, capacity, of; representing) followed by a noun:

Le tuvieron por espía.	*They took him for a spy.*
como músico	*as a musician*
Le fusilaron por traidor.	*They shot him as a traitor.*

- Before the object of **tener** or verbs meaning *to wear*, unless the oneness of the object is stressed or it is highly individualised:

Tengo coche.	*I've got a car.*
Ella viste falda azul.	*She's wearing a blue dress.*

but:

No tienen **un** hijo sino cuatro.	*They haven't got one child, but four.*
El vestía **un** traje muy de moda.	*He was wearing a very trendy suit.*

Similarly with **con**:

Escribes con bolígrafo.	*You write with a biro.*

- After **sin**:

sin duda	*without a doubt*

- In a number of set phrases:

a precio fijo	*at a fixed price*
a gran distancia	*at a great distance*
estar de buen humor	*to be in a good mood*

▼ *Use of the neuter article* lo

- Before an adjective, participle or adjectival phrase to form a kind of abstract noun:

Lo interesante es que. . .	*What is interesting is that. . .*
Ella cree **lo** mismo.	*She thinks the same.*
desde **lo** alto de la colina	*from the top of the hill*
Es **lo** de siempre.	*It's the same old story.*
Siento **lo** ocurrido.	*I'm sorry about what has happened.*

When an adjective or participle is used in this kind of expression it is always in the masculine singular form.

- Before an adjective or adverb followed by **que** to translate *how* in exclamations:

¡Mira **lo** rápido que corre!	*Look how fast he's running!*
¿Has visto **lo** cansada que está?	*Have you seen how tired she is?*
Yo sé **lo** difíciles que son.	*I know how difficult they are.*

Note that here the adjective does agree with the noun to which it refers.

- In certain phrases, such as:

por lo menos	*at least*	por lo tanto	*therefore*
a lo mejor	*probably*	a lo largo de	*along*
a lo lejos	*in the distance*	por lo visto	*apparently*

▼ **Activity 2** *Articles*

Translate the articles in brackets and make them agree according to the gender of the nouns which follow:

Estoy pasando (a) día en (a) hotel en (the) centro de (the) cuidad. Desde (the) balcón puedo ver (the) plaza mayor, que tiene (a) fuente grande y (some) palmeras. A (one) lado está la catedral y a (the) otro lado hay (a) parque donde (the) gente está tomando (the) sol. A (the) fondo, a (the) pie de (the) montañas y detrás de (the) universidad, se puede ver (the) aeropuerto. Puedo ver (a) avión aterrizar. En (the) cielo hay (some) nubes.

▼▼▼
ADJECTIVES
describing people, places and things

Adjectives are words which give us more information about nouns. Adjectives in Spanish change their endings ('agree') according to the gender of the noun to which they refer, and according to whether the noun is singular or plural.

▼ Agreement

la casa blanca — *the white house*
Los libros son interesantes. — *The books are interesting.*

If an adjective is agreeing with two or more singular nouns of the same gender, it has a plural ending of that gender:

la geografía y la historia españolas — *Spanish geography and history*

If an adjective is agreeing with both a masculine and a feminine noun, it has a masculine plural ending:

Los chicos y las chicas están contentos. — *The boys and girls are happy.*

▼ Feminine forms

- Adjectives ending in -o in the masculine singular change to -a for the feminine singular:

rojo – roja

- The following groups add -a:

Adjectives relating to places and ending in a consonant.

Those ending in -án, -ín, -ón, -or (except the irregular comparatives):

español	– española	barcelonés	– barcelonesa
holgazán	– holgazana	burlón	– burlona
encantador	– encantadora		

....

● The rest are the same whether masculine or feminine:

el general **belga** – la monja **belga**, el lápiz **verde** – la pluma **verde**, el estudiante **feliz** – la enfermera **feliz**, el cónsul **iraquí** – la embajada **iraquí**, el **mejor** capítulo – la **mejor** novela

▼ Plural forms

● With adjectives ending in an unstressed vowel add -**s**:

verde – verde**s**, tonto – tonto**s**, buena – buena**s**

● To those ending in a stressed vowel or a consonant add -**es**:

hindú – hindú**es**, marroquí – marroquí**es**, regular – regular**es**, fácil – fácil**es**, francés – frances**es**

Because of these rules, adjectives which add an -**a** to form the feminine singular (see page 19) will have masculine plural ending -**es** and the feminine plural ending -**as**:

español**es** – español**as**, encantador**es** – encantador**as**

The usual spelling and accent rules apply when forming the feminine and plural:

inglés – ingle**sa**, ingle**ses**, ingle**sas**; feliz – feli**ces**

■ **Adjectives which never change in the feminine or plural**

These are, in fact, other parts of speech, such as nouns, which are used as adjectives:

coches **cama**   *sleeping-cars*

The same applies to several names of colours:

las corbatas **rosa**   *the pink ties*

It also applies to adjectives consisting of more than one word:

los coches **azul oscuro**   *the dark blue cars*

In the case of some well used compound nouns this rule is now being broken, for example:

lenguas **madres**   *mother tongues*
ciudades **satélites**   *satellite towns*

▼ Shortened forms

The following adjectives drop the final -o before a masculine singular noun: **bueno, malo, alguno, ninguno, primero, tercero, postrero, uno**:

el **tercer** día, el **primer** libro, **algún** día, un **buen** jefe

Uno does the same when it is part of a compound number:

veintiún árboles

- **Santo** changes to **San**, except with saints' names beginning **Do-** or **To-**:

San Miguel, **Santo** Domingo, **Santo** Tomás

Santa is not affected: **Santa** María

- **Grande** usually becomes **gran** before singular nouns of either gender:

El **gran** presidente, la **gran** actriz

- **Ciento** becomes **cien** except before a number smaller than itself:

cien mil	*100,000*	**cien** barcos	*a hundred boats*
Compró **cien**.	*He bought a hundred.*		

but:

ciento dos   *a hundred and two*

- **Cualquiera** and **cualesquiera** usually drop the final -a before nouns of either gender:

cualquier mes, **cualquier** situación

▼ Activity 1   *Agreement of adjectives*

Make the adjectives in brackets agree with the noun they describe:

En el (primero) almacén que visitaron los turistas (japonés) compraron una camisa (azul), unos calcetines (rojo) (oscuro), unos zapatos (marrón), una chaqueta (gris), dos camisetas (blanco) y una (grande) toalla (verde).

▼ Position of adjectives

Adjectives in Spanish normally follow the noun to which they belong, but this rule is often broken to achieve a particular effect as well as in the cases given below.

▼ *Adjectives following a noun*

- Defining adjectives (such as colours, nationalities, those describing physical features, etc.):

los vinos **alemanes**	*German wines*
la torre **alta**	*the high tower*

- Compound adjectives (those consisting of more than one word) and usually those accompanied by an adverb:

una familia **bastante rica**	*quite a rich family*

- A number of common adjectives, such as **bueno**, **malo**, **joven**, **viejo**, **grande** and **pequeño** may be used before or after the noun.

They generally come *before* in set expressions and *after* for emphasis:

Hace **mal** tiempo.	*The weather is bad.*
mala suerte	*bad luck*
una película **mala**	*a (really) bad film*

See also irregular comparatives page 25.

▼ *Adjectives before the noun*

- Possessive adjectives *my, your*, demonstrative adjectives *this, that*, numbers (with a few exceptions – see page 137).

- Other adjectives of quantity such as **alguno**, **cada**, **demás**, **bastante**, **demasiado**, **mucho**, **poco**, **cuanto**, **todo**, **ninguno**, **otro**, **tal**:

cada semana	*each week*

Note: **otro** normally comes before any numeral or adjective of quantity used with it:

otras muchas mujeres	*many other women*

Alguno precedes the noun unless the meaning is negative:

algunos caballos	*some horses*

but:

sin dinero **alguno**	*without any money*
(See page 68.)	

• Adjectives used figuratively (not literally):

un **viejo** amigo mío	*an old friend of mine*

but:

un coche **viejo**	*an old car*

▼ *Position when two adjectives are used*
When both adjectives are of equal importance they usually follow the noun and are joined by **y**:

un señor **guapo y simpático**	*a nice good-looking man*

Otherwise the adjective less closely related to the noun usually comes first:

una **hermosa** playa andaluza	*a beautiful Andalucian beach*

▼ *Position and meaning*
Some adjectives change their meaning according to their position.

For example:

	before noun	after noun
antiguo	*former*	*old, ancient*
cierto	*a certain (unspecified)**	*definite*
diferente	*various*	*different*
grande	*great, grand*	*big*
medio	*half**	*average*
mismo	*same*	*-self, precisely*
nuevo	*new, another, fresh*	*brand new*
pobre	*poor (unfortunate)*	*poor (penniless)*
puro	*sheer, mere*	*pure (untainted)*
varios	*several*	*various, different*
viejo	*old (long known, etc.)*	*old (aged)*

*See page 138.

───

■ **Adjectives used as nouns**
Adjectives in Spanish are sometimes used like nouns. They
agree in the usual way:

¿Qué bufanda le gusta? Me gusta **la azul.**	*Which scarf do you like? I like the blue one.*
un barco inglés y **uno francés**	*an English boat and a French one*

(Note that **uno** does not drop its **o** when used in this way.)

los ricos	*the rich*
la vieja	*the old woman*

───

▼ Comparisons with adjectives

* To say *more* interesting, easi*er*, etc. (the comparative form of the adjective), use **más** in front of the regular form of the adjective.

* To say *less* interesting, *less* easy, etc. use **menos** in front of the regular form of the adjective.

* To say *most* interesting, easi*est*, etc. (the superlative form of the adjective), use **el más/la más/los más/las más** in front of the regular form of the adjective.

* To say *least* interesting, *least* easy, etc. use **el menos/la menos/los menos/las menos** in front of the regular form of the adjective.

The adjectives and articles agree in the usual way and **que** translates *than*:

Estos ejercicios son fáciles, pero el que hice ayer es **el más fácil** de todos.	*These exercises are easy, but the one I did yesterday is the easiest of all.*
El edificio nuevo es **menos feo que** el viejo.	*The new building is less ugly than the old one.*
Su abuela es la mujer la **más vieja** de la ciudad.	*His grandmother is the oldest woman in the town.*

Note: in after a superlative is translated by **de**.

Irregular comparatives

Just like *good – better – best* in English, there are a few Spanish adjectives with irregular comparative and superlative forms:

bueno	mejor	el mejor	*good*	*better*	*(the) best*
malo	peor	el peor	*bad*	*worse*	*(the) worst*
grande	mayor	el mayor		*(see below)*	
pequeño	menor	el menor		*(see below)*	

Mejor and **peor** are usually placed before the noun:

la **mejor** película	*the best film*
el **peor** vino	*the worst wine*

Más (or **menos**) **grande** and **más** (or **menos**) **pequeño** are used mostly for physical size:

Esta vaca es **más grande** que la otra.	*This cow is bigger than the other one.*
Aquel cuchillo es **el más pequeño**.	*That knife over there is the smallest.*

Mayor and **menor** are used above all for age, degrees of importance and abstract size. They come before the noun when expressing degrees of importance, abstract size or relative quantities:

No cabe la **menor** duda.	*There is not the slightest doubt.*
la **mayor** parte	*the greater part, the majority*

and after the noun when expressing age or seniority and in a few set expressions:

Miguel es el hijo **mayor**.	*Miguel is the eldest son.*
la calle **mayor**	*the High Street*
la plaza **mayor**	*the main square*

Other irregular comparatives:

anterior	*previous*		posterior	*subsequent, later*
exterior	*external, exterior*		interior	*internal, inside*
superior	*upper*		inferior	*lower*

These usually come after the noun:

la semana **anterior**	*the previous week*
las habitaciones **interiores**	*the inside rooms*

The absolute superlative (*very, most, extremely,* etc. + adjective)
This may be formed by adding -ísimo to the adjective after
removing any final vowel, e.g.:

viejo	viejísimo		poco	poquísimo
difícil	dificilísimo		feroz	ferocísimo
rápido	rapidísimo		largo	larguísimo

Notice the accent and that the usual spelling changes (see page 1–6).

Es un coche **rapidísimo**.	*It is an extremely fast car.*
la leonesa **ferocísima**	*the very fierce lioness*

There are some irregular forms, e.g.:

amable	amabilísimo
nuevo	novísimo

Alternatively, **muy** (*very*) may be placed in front of the adjective:

La novela es **muy** interesante.	*The novel is very interesting.*

except in the case of **mucho**:

Le gusta **muchísimo**.	*He likes it very much.*

mucho translates *very* on its own:

¿Está enojada? Sí, pero no **mucho**.	*Is she annoyed? Yes, but not very.*

▼ Activity 2   *Comparisons using adjectives*

Complete the following sentences translating the words in brackets:

a ¿Qué niños son (*the tallest*)?
  Los niños de su hermano son (*taller than*) los de su primo, pero los
  tuyos son (*the tallest*).
b ¿Qué fruta es (*the least expensive*)?
  Los plátanos son (*less expensive than*) las naranjas, pero las manzanas
  son (*the least expensive*).
c ¿Qué platos prefieres?
  Los platos azules son (*better than*) los rojos, pero (*the worst*) son los
  amarillos.

▼ Possessive adjectives (weak forms)

These are the words like *my*, *your* and *their* which are used to show that something belongs to someone. In Spanish these words behave just like other adjectives, agreeing with the noun they describe.

	singular		plural	
	masculine	*feminine*	*masculine*	*feminine*
my	mi	mi	mis	mis
your (of **tú**)	tu	tu	tus	tus
his, her, its *your* (of **Vd.**)	su	su	sus	sus
our	nuestro	nuestra	nuestros	nuestras
your (of **vosotros**)	vuestro	vuestra	vuestros	vuestras
their *your* (of **Vds.**)	su	su	sus	sus

These weak forms always come before the noun:

mis camisas	*my shirts*
nuestro perro	*our dog*
Ella necesita **sus** cuadernos.	*She needs her exercise books.*

As you can see from the table above, **su** and **sus** can mean *his, her, its your* (of **Vd.**, **Vds.**) or *their*, so it is often necessary to add extra words to make the meaning clear unless it is obvious from the context (as in the last example above). This is done in the following way:

Tengo **la** pluma **de él**.	*I have his pen.*
instead of : Tengo **su** pluma.	
Vimos **al** padre **de ellos**.	*We saw their father.*
instead of: Vimos a **su** padre.	
Conoce a **los** hermanos **de Vd**.	*He knows your brothers.*
instead of: Conoce a **sus** hermanos.	

Alternatively, **su** and **sus** can be used instead of the definite article:

Conoce a **sus** hermanos **de Vd**.

When parts of the body or pieces of clothing are the object of a verb, possession is shown by one of the following:

- by a reflexive pronoun if they belong to the subject:

Se quitó el impermeable.　　　*She took her (own) raincoat off.*
Me he roto la pierna.　　　*I have broken my leg.*

- by an indirect object pronoun:

Tu madre **te** lavará la cara.　　*Your mother will wash your face.*
Le aprietan los zapatos.　　　*His shoes are pinching him.*

Where ownership is clear, the object pronoun is frequently omitted:

Abrió la boca.　　　*She opened her mouth.*

▼ Possessive adjectives (strong forms)

	singular		plural	
	masculine	*feminine*	*masculine*	*feminine*
my/mine	mío	mía	míos	mías
your(s) (of **tú**)	tuyo	tuya	tuyos	tuyas
his, her(s), its *your(s)* (of **Vd.**)	suyo	suya	suyos	suyas
our(s)	nuestro	nuestra	nuestros	nuestras
your(s) (of **vosotros**)	vuestro	vuestra	vuestros	vuestras
their(s) *your(s)* (of **Vds.**)	suyo	suya	suyos	suyas

They agree in the same way as the weak forms above (page 27) but come after the noun or pronoun they are describing or after the verb **ser**.

They are used:

- for emphasis; note that the noun described is preceded by the definite article:

La finca **suya** es enorme.　　*His farm is enormous.*
¿Has encontrado **el** anillo **mío**?　*Have you found my ring?*

- after a noun when addressing people figuratively or literally:

hijo **mío**	*my son*
¡Dios **mío**!	*My God!*
Muy señor **mío**:	*Dear Sir,* (in letters)

- in the following expressions:

un amigo **mío**	*a friend of mine*
algo **tuyo**	*something of yours*

(Note that **de** is not used.)

- after the verb **ser**:

Este lápiz es **nuestro**.	*This pencil is ours.*

For emphasis the definite article can be placed in front:

Este lápiz es **el** nuestro, ése es **el** vuestro.	*This pencil is ours, that one is yours.*

It is often necessary to use an alternative to **suyo, suya**, etc. to make the meaning clear:

el amigo **de ella**	*her friend*
(*instead of* el amigo **suyo**)	

Este gato es **de Vd.**	*This cat is yours.*
or:	
Este gato es **el de Vd.** (more emphatic)	

▼ Activity 3   *Possessive adjectives*

Complete the following sentences translating the words in brackets and making the ownership clear in the case of third person forms:

a ¿De quién son estas cosas?
Los lápices son (*mine*), la tinta es (*yours – relating to* tú) y las plumas son (*hers*).

b ¿Habéis terminado (*your – relating to* vosotros) trabajo?
Nosotros hemos terminado (*our*) ejercicios, pero él no ha escrito (*his*) composición todavía.

c ¿Son (*yours – relating to* Vds.) estas maletas?
Las maletas verdes son (*ours*) y la pequeña es (*mine*), pero las azules allí son (*theirs – relating to* men) y las rojas son (*theirs – relating to* women).

d ¿Cuál es (*your – relating to* tú) bicicleta?
Esta es (*my*) bicicleta. La otra es (*his*).

▼ Demonstrative adjectives

		masculine	*feminine*
this		este	esta
these		estos	estas
that	far from speaker but	ese	esa
those	near person addressed	esos	esas
that	far from both speaker	aquel	aquella
those	and person addressed	aquellos	aquellas

The demonstrative adjectives are usually put before the noun to which they refer:

Esa revista no me interesa pero este periódico sí.

That magazine doesn't interest me but this newspaper does.

▼ Activity 4   *Demonstrative adjectives*

Complete the following dialogue using the appropriate form of *este*:

- ¿Qué has comprado?
- He comprado . . . postales y . . . helado.
- Y tú, ¿qué has comprado?
- Yo he comprado . . . castañuelas y . . . mantilla.

ADVERBS
describing where, when and how something is done

Adverbs are the words used to describe verbs, adjectives or even other adverbs.

▼ Formation

Most adverbs are formed by adding -**mente** to the feminine form of the adjective:

adj. masc.	adj. fem.	adverb
franco	franca	francamente
fácil	fácil	fácilmente

If the adjective has an accent it stays in the same place on the adverb:

fácil   fácilmente

When two or more such adverbs are used together, the -**mente** is omitted from all but the last:

Se lo dijo **severa** pero **cortésmente.**   *He told him so severely but politely.*

As the adverbs ending in -**mente** are often rather long and clumsy, adjectives are frequently used instead:

Los compramos muy **barato.**   *We bought them very cheaply.*
Ella corre **rápido.**   *She runs quickly.*

In some cases they agree:

Vivieron **contentos.**   *They lived happily.*

Alternatively, a phrase can be used:

con frecuencia	*frequently*	por fin	*finally*
		con cuidado	*carefully*

de $\left\{ \begin{array}{l} \text{una manera} \\ \text{un modo} \end{array} \right\}$ muy audaz   *very audaciously*

▼ *Irregular adverbs*

bueno	good	bien	well
malo	bad	mal	badly

recientemente shortens to **recién** before a past participle:

los **recién** casados	the newly married couple

In Spanish America it may be used at other times as well:

Recién salió.	He left a short while ago.

▼ Activity 1   *Forming adverbs*

Make these adjectives into adverbs: final, perfecto, exacto, feroz, triste.

▼ Position of adverbs

Adverbs usually follow the verb which they describe. However, they can go in front of the verb instead for special emphasis:

Siempre está hablando por teléfono con su novio.	She's **always** talking on the phone to her boyfriend.
Conocemos **bien** a Rosalía.	We know Rosalia well.

If an adverb is describing an adjective or another adverb, then it precedes it:

Vive **muy** cerca.	He lives very near.
Son **demasiado** caros.	They are too expensive.

When any of the following adverbs are used with another adverb, they always go first:

allí mismo	right there	**mañana** temprano	early tomorrow
aquí cerca	near here		

▼ Activity 2   *Position of adverbs*

Place the adverbs in brackets in the correct position in the sentence:

a Pedro está enamorado de Patricia. (locamente)
b El guía lo tradujo bien. (bastante)
c El conductor fue herido en el accidente. (gravemente)
d Se levanta a las siete. (normalmente)
e El cumpleaños de su abuelo es mismo. (hoy)

▼ Comparisons with adverbs

To compare actions in Spanish, you put **más** or **menos** before the adverb. **Que** usually translates *than*.

Pedro corre **más** rápido.	*Pedro runs faster.*
El que corre **más** rápido . . .	*The one who runs faster/the fastest . . .*
Luisa corre **más** rápido **que** José.	*Luisa runs faster than José.*

The neuter article **lo** is added before a superlative when there is extra information:

Antonio corrió **lo** más rápido que pudo.   *Antonio ran as fast as he could.*

Irregular comparison

bien	mejor	(lo) mejor		*well*	*better*	*(the) best*
mal	peor	(lo) peor		*badly*	*worse*	*(the) worst*
mucho	más	(lo) más		*much*	*more*	*(the) most*
poco	menos	(lo) menos		*little*	*less*	*(the) least*

Rosa canta **mejor** que María.	*Rosa sings better than Maria.*
Paco come **menos que** Enrique.	*Paco eats less than Enrique.*

▼ Activity 3   *Comparisons using adverbs*

Complete the following sentences using one of these phrases: **más, menos, mejor, lo mejor, lo peor**:

a Yo no necesito gafas. Puedo ver . . . que tú.
b Le daré el libro a mi sobrino porque le interesa . . . que a mi sobrina.
c Pepa ganó el premio porque recitó el poema . . . .
d ¡Toca la guitarra . . . alto, Manolo! Estás haciendo demasiado ruido.
e Andrés nada mal, pero Felipe nada . . . de la clase.

▼ *Other expressions of comparison*

Más de and **menos de** are used before numbers:

Tiene **más de** cinco hermanas. *He has more than five sisters.*

Note that this does not apply to the expressions **no . . . más que** (*only*):

No tenemos **más que** cien pesetas. *We only have a hundred pesetas.*

• *As . . . as* tan . . . como

Esta casa es **tan** moderna **como** aquélla. *This house is as modern as that one.*

• *As much/many . . . as* tanto . . . como

Vds. no beben **tanto como** ellos. *You do not drink as much as them.*

Tanto agrees when used as an adjective:

Esta sala no tiene **tantos** cuadros **como** ésa. *This room has not got as many pictures as that one.*

• *The more/less . . . the more/less* cuanto más/menos . . . tanto más/menos

Cuanto and **tanto** agree when used as adjectives:

Cuanto más come, **tanto más** engorda. *The more he eats, the fatter he gets.*

Cuantos más coches venden, **tanto más** feliz será el gerente. *The more cars they sell, the happier the manager will be.*

• *So . . . that* tan . . . que

Estaba **tan** enfermo **que** le llevaron al hospital. *He was so ill that they took him to hospital.*

• *More and more/less and less* cada vez más/menos

Está trabajando **cada vez menos** en la oficina. *He is working less and less in the office.*

A ella le gusta la música **cada vez más**. *She likes music more and more.*

• *Too (much/many) . . . to* demasiado . . . para

Es **demasiado** temprano **para** cenar. *It is too early to have supper.*

Demasiado agrees when used as an adjective:

Tiene **demasiada** inteligencia **para** dejarse engañar así.

He is too intelligent to allow himself to be deceived like that.

• *Enough . . . to* bastante . . . para

No se siente **bastante** bien **para** ir a la reunión.

He does not feel well enough to go to the party.

Bastante agrees when used as an adjective:

Tiene **bastantes** ahorros **para** comprar la finca.

She has enough savings to buy the farm.

Bastante also means *quite, quite a bit, quite a few*:

Hace **bastante** calor.
Había **bastante** ruido.

It is quite hot.
There was quite a bit of noise

In this context, when followed by a verb the construction is **bastante** + **que** + infinitive:

Tengo **bastantes** cosas **que** hacer.

I have quite a few things to do.

▼ Activity 4   *Other comparisons*

Complete the following sentences using one of these phrases (none of which can be used more than once):

tanto como, cuanto más . . . tanto más, más de, más . . . que, bastante, bastante . . . para, tan . . . como, tantos . . . como, tan . . . que, cada vez menos.

a   Vd. ha gastado . . . 10.000 pesetas.
b   Está . . . cansado . . . no puede correr más.
c   La cocina estaba . . . limpia.
d   María no parece . . . enferma . . . Isabel.
e   Ella no tiene . . . caballos . . . su amiga.
f   . . . trabajaba, . . . se cansaba.
g   El bebé duerme . . . ahora.
h   ¿Vd. tiene . . . dinero . . . comprar los billetes?
i   Llueve . . . en el sur . . . en el norte.
j   Eduardo no juega al fútbol . . . antes.

PRONOUNS
replacing nouns

▼ Personal pronouns

Personal pronouns stand instead of nouns which refer to people or things. Here is a table of personal pronouns in Spanish. Their meanings and uses are explained below.

	subject	direct object	indirect object	reflexive
	(I, etc.)	*(me, etc.)*	*(to me, etc.)*	*(myself, etc.)*
I	yo	me	me	me
*you**	tú	te	te	te
he, it (masc.)	él	lo		
she, it (fem.)	ella	la	le	se
*you**	usted (Vd.)	lo, la		
we (masc.)	nosotros			
we (all fem.)	nosotras	nos	nos	nos
you (masc.)*	vosotros			
you (all fem.)*	vosotras	os	os	
they (masc.)	ellos	los		
they (all fem.)	ellas	las	les	se
*you**	ustedes (Vds.)	los, las		

* For the translation of *you* into Spanish see pages 8–9.

Nosotros, vosotros, ellos, los, nos and **os** may also be used for mixed groups of both sexes. **Le** may also be used instead of **lo** and **les** instead of **los** when referring to male people.

▼ Subject pronouns

A subject pronoun replaces a noun which is the subject – i.e. doing the action – of the verb. In Spanish, unlike English, you usually omit the subject pronoun altogether because the ending of the verb shows whether the subject is *you*, *I* or *they*, etc.:

Eres estudiante.	*You are a student.*
Somos turistas.	*We are tourists.*

Subject pronouns are used for emphasis or when the verb ending does not make the subject clear:

Yo soy español, pero **él** es mejicano.   *I am Spanish, but he is Mexican.*

Vd. and **Vds.** should, however, always be put in:

¿Qué desea **Vd.**?   *What would you like?*

The words *it* or *they*, when referring to things, are never translated when they are the subject:

¿Qué es? Es una oveja.   *What is it? It's a sheep.*
¿Qué son? Son corbatas.   *What are they? They're ties.*

▼ Other pronouns

• Object pronouns
An object pronoun takes the place of a noun which is the object – i.e. receiving the action – of the verb. There are two kinds of objects and object pronouns: direct and indirect. In the sentence below, Jane is the subject, the book is the direct object and Peter is the indirect object:

Jane gave the book to Peter. or *Jane gave Peter the book.*

If the nouns in this sentence are all replaced by pronouns, the sentence becomes:

She gave it to him. or *She gave him it.*

• Reflexive pronouns
These are special pronouns used to translate *-self*. Reflexive verbs are explained on pages 107–11.

▼ Position and order of subject and object pronouns

The order of object pronouns

This is always the same:

reflexive – indirect – direct (R – I – D)

Word order in statements

1	2	3	4	5	6	7
subject	1st negative	reflexive	indirect object	direct object	verb	2nd negative

Examples:

1 5 6
El me ve.   *He sees me.*

  1   3   6
Nosotros nos lavamos.   *We wash ourselves.*

1 4 5 6
Yo te lo he dado.   *I've given it to you.*

1 5 6
Ella los está llamando.   *She is calling them.*

1 2 4 5   6
Vds. no me la mostraron.   *You didn't show it to me.*

   1   2   5 6
Vosotros nunca los podéis encontrar.   *You can never find them.*

1 2 4 5 6   7
Tú no nos lo prestas nunca.   *You never lend it to us.*

This does not apply where an infinitive or present participle is being used on its own – see below.

The negatives are explained more fully on pages 67–71.

Word order with infinitives (*to do* forms) and present participles (-*ing* forms)

When an infinitive or present participle is being used on its own, the object pronouns are joined on to the end of it as follows:

afeitar**se**	*to shave (oneself)*	comiéndo**lo**	*eating it*
enviándo**melo**	*sending it to me*	dár**telo**	*to give it to you*

Accents are required to show the stress, except where only one pronoun is added to the infinitive.

Where an infinitive or present participle is used after another verb, the object pronouns can go either before the first verb or after the second:

Me lo quiere dar. ⎤ Quiere dár**melo**. ⎦	*He wants to give it to me.*
Le voy a escribir. ⎤ Voy a escribir**le**. ⎦	*I'm going to write to him.*
Lo está bebiendo. ⎤ Está bebiéndo**lo** ⎦	*He is drinking it.*

Word order with negative commands (*Don't . . .*)

Object pronouns are joined onto the end of the command form (or 'imperative'):

¡Dá**melo**!	*Give it to me!*

If the command is negative, they precede it in the usual order:

No **me lo** des.	*Don't give it to me.*

The subject pronoun always follows the imperative if it is needed for emphasis:

¡Oye **tú**!	*Hey, you!*

Word order in questions

To form a question, the subject pronoun, if needed, may be placed either at the beginning of the phrase or immediately after the verb. Object pronouns stay in the same place as usual:

Vd. ¿cuándo llegó aquí? ⎤ ¿Cuándo llegó **Vd**. aquí? ⎦	*When did you arrive here?*
¿Han pagado **Vds**.?	*Have you paid?*
¿Cuándo me lo puede hacer **Vd**.?	*When can you do it for me?*

Note that two verbs used together may never be separated. Quite often questions have the same word order as statements, but you can tell the difference by the question marks in writing and by the rising intonation in speech:

¿Ella ha estado enferma?	*Has she been ill?*

Using two 3rd person object pronouns together

Where two 3rd person object pronouns are used together, the first one always changes to **se** to make the phrase easier to pronounce:

Yo **se** lo doy. ⎰	*for:* Yo **le** lo doy.	*I give it to him/her/you* (**Vd**.).
	or: Yo **les** lo doy.	*I give it to them/you* (**Vds**.).

Clarification of 3rd person indirect object pronouns
Because **le** can mean *to him, to her, to you* (**Vd**.)
     les can mean *to them* (masc. or fem.) or *to you* (**Vds.**)
     se can mean any of the above

to make the meaning clear, if necessary, **a él** *to him*, **a ella** *to her*, etc. can be added to the phrase, usually after the verb:

Yo le escribo **a ella**.	*I write to her.*
Yo se lo doy **a ellos**.	*I give it to them.*

Note that the indirect object pronoun is still used even though it no longer seems necessary.

▼ Some special points about object pronouns

- **Le** is used in many parts of the Spanish-speaking world instead of **lo** when referring to a person, not a thing. **Les** is likewise used instead of **los**, but in fewer areas:

Le/lo veo mañana.	*I'm seeing him tomorrow.*
Les/los conocimos en Madrid.	*We met them in Madrid.*

- The indirect object pronouns often translate *for me*, etc. as well as *to me*, etc.:

Te ha comprado un regalo.	*He has bought a present for you.*
Me lo preparará esta tarde.	*He will prepare it for me this afternoon.*

The indirect object is often disguised in English, thus the first sentence could also be translated: *He has bought you a present.* Make sure that you distinguish between the direct and the indirect objects before translating a sentence into Spanish.

- Where a noun object precedes the verb in Spanish it must also be represented by the appropriate object pronoun:

La región **la** conocemos muy bien, pero la ciudad no.	*We know the region well, but not the city.*
Al tío **le** visitamos ayer.	*We visited the uncle yesterday.*

This rule is often applied when a noun follows the verb as an indirect object, although in this case it is not grammatically necessary:

Le va a telefonear **a María**.	*She is going to phone Maria.*

- Indirect object pronouns are usually used instead of possessive adjectives with parts of the body or clothing (see page 28):

Me duele el brazo.   *My arm aches.*

▼ Activity 1   *Pronouns*

Convert the words underlined into pronouns and place them in the appropriate position in the sentence, making sure that the meaning of *se* forms is clear, as explained on pages 39–40:

a   Vds. vieron <u>la capital</u>.
b   ¡Prepare <u>la comida para nosotros</u>!
c   El jefe ¿cuándo explicó <u>el problema a su cliente</u>?
d   María está mostrando <u>los cuadros a tus hermanos</u>.
e   ¡No des <u>los huesos al perro</u>!
f   Ella va a escribir <u>el poema para mí</u>.
g   Nosotros no nos lavamos <u>las manos</u>.
h   José tradujo <u>la carta para ti</u>.
i   Ha comprado <u>los regalos para vosotras</u>.
j   Puedo devolver <u>el libro</u> mañana.

▼ Reflexive pronouns

The use of these is covered on pages 107–11. See also below.

▼ Pronouns after prepositions

- After a preposition (a word such as **para**, **de**, **bajo**) the pronouns to use are the same as the subject pronouns, except for **mí** (*me*) and **ti** (*you* singular):

para **mí**	*for me*	detrás de **nosotros**	*behind us*
hacia **él**	*towards him*	enfrente de vosotros	*opposite you*

Note the accent on **mí** to distinguish it from **mi** which means *my*.

- Reflexive pronouns used after a preposition:

Mí, ti, nosotros and **vosotros** as above and **sí** for all 3rd person pronouns:

Estaba leyendo para **mí**.	*I was reading to myself.*
El está hablando para **sí**.	*He is talking to himself.*

- **Con** combines only with **mí, ti** and **sí** to form **conmigo, contigo, consigo**:

Llegaron **con ella**.	*They arrived with her.*
Charlaron **conmigo**.	*They chatted with me.*

- A subject pronoun is used after the following prepositions instead of **mí** and **ti**:

entre *between, among;* **hasta, incluso** *even, including;* **salvo, menos** *except;* **según** *according to* (the same applies to the conjunctions **y, o** and **que**):

entre **tú** y **yo**	*between you and me*
hasta **yo**	*even I*

- **Ello** *it, that* is used after a preposition when referring to an idea or statement and not a specific noun:

Con respecto a **ello** . . .	*As far as that is concerned . . .*

- These pronouns used after prepositions may also be used for emphasis or to make it clearer who the object is:

A mí no me gusta, pero a **él*** sí.	*I don't like it, but he does.*
¿Qué te pasa a **ti**?	*What's the matter with you?*

*A él, de él, do not contract as is the case with the definite article (see page 14).

▼ Relative pronouns: *who, what, which, etc.*

	singular	plural
who (subject)	que	que
whom (direct object)	que* a quien	que* a quienes
to whom	a quien	a quienes
of whom	de que de quien	de que de quienes
whose	cuyo	cuyo

*Que is used more frequently than **a quien(es)**.

	singular and plural
which (subject) (that)	que
which (direct object) (that)	que
to which	a que
of which	de que
whose	cuyo

These forms may refer to people or things of either gender.

- **Cuyo** agrees adjectivally with the noun it qualifies, NOT with the owner:

El amigo en **cuya** casa nos hospedábamos . . .	*The friend in whose house we were staying . . .*

- The relative pronoun may never be left out in Spanish although we can sometimes omit it in English:

el médico **que** (**a quien**) vio ayer	*the doctor (whom) he saw yesterday*
la casa **que** están construyendo	*the house (which) they are building*

- When the relative pronoun is separated from the word to which it refers, or if it is unclear, it is replaced by **el cual** or **el que**, both of which must agree:

El perro de mi hermana, **el cual** (*or* **el que**) se llama Pepito, es negro.	*My sister's dog, which is called Pepito, is black.*

(**Que** would mean that the sister, not the dog, is called Pepito.)

- **Que** and **quien** are generally used after the prepositions **a**, **de**, **con** and **en**. After other prepositions, **el que** or **el cual**, etc. are used instead:

El piso **en que** ella vive es moderno.	*The flat she lives in is modern.*
la calle **por la cual** está corriendo el chico	*the street the boy is running along*

- The expressions *he who, she who, the one who/which*, etc. are translated by **el que**, etc.:

Esta moto es **la que** quiero comprar.	*This motorbike is the one I want to buy.*
¿Conoces el edificio – **el que** está enfrente del banco?	*Do you know the building – the one which is opposite the bank?*

Quien may also be used to translate *he who*, etc. and also *whoever*:

Ella era **quien** fue a Alemania.	She was the one who went to Germany.
Quien dice eso debe estar loco.	Whoever says that must be mad.

- The neuter **lo que** translates *what* or *which* when referring to an idea, statement or undefined noun or activity:

No sabe **lo que** estáis haciendo.	He doesn't know what you are doing.
Estaba solo, **lo que** les pareció muy raro.	He was alone, which they thought very strange.

In the last type of expression **lo cual** may also be used.

All that is translated by **todo lo que**.

All who, all those which are translated by **todos los que** or **todas las que**:

Explicó **todo lo que** pasó.	He explained all that happened.
Todos los que fueron a la fiesta se divirtieron mucho.	All who went to the party enjoyed themselves very much.

- **El** (etc.) **de** translates *the one of, that of, X's one*:

esta foto y **la de** su hija	this photo and that of his daughter
El programa de hoy es mejor que **el de** ayer.	Today's programme is better than yesterday's.

▼ Activity 2   *Relative pronouns*

Complete the following sentences using the appropriate pronoun:

a   El avión en . . . viajó a Nueva York llegó tarde.
b   Busco los lápices . . . te presté.
c   El director a . . . llamaste no está en la oficina.
d   No entendieron todo . . . les dijo.
e   El profesor . . . estudiantes están allí enseña geografía.
f   ¿Qué tazas rompiste? . . . estaban cerca de la ventana.
g   Trajo sus niñas y . . . su hermana.
h   Conozco los jóvenes con . . . fuiste a París.
i   El río por . . . estaba nadando es muy sucio.
j   ¿Sabéis . . . han escrito en su carta?

▼ Possessive pronouns

These are the words like *mine* and *yours* which show that
something belongs to someone. Possessive pronouns in Spanish
are the same as the strong forms of the possessive adjectives (see
page 28) and are always accompanied by the definite article:

nuestra oficina y **la suya** *or* **la de ella** *our office and hers*
tus bolígrafos y **los míos**   *your biros and mine*

▼ Activity 3   *Possessive pronouns*

Complete the following sentences translating the words in brackets:

a ¿Has encontrado nuestras sandalias?
  He encontrado (*mine*) pero no (*yours – relating to* tú) .
b ¿Habéis terminado vuestros libros?
  Nosotros hemos terminado (*ours*) pero ellos no han terminado (*theirs*).
c ¿Qué paquete pesa más?
  (*Mine*) pesa más que (*hers*).
d ¿Ha reservado nuestra habitación?
  Sí, ha reservado (*yours – relating to* vosotros) y (*theirs*) también.
e ¿Qué cuadros preferiste? Me gustaron más (*hers*) que (*his*).

▼ Demonstrative pronouns

These are used when *this (one)*, *that (one)*, *these (ones)*, *those (ones)*
stand alone without a noun.

	masculine	*feminine*	*neuter*		*masculine*	*feminine*
this	éste	ésta	esto	*these*	éstos	éstas
that {	ése	ésa	eso	*those* {	ésos	ésas
{	aquél	aquélla	aquello	{	aquéllos	aquéllas

The difference between **ése** and **aquél** is the same as between the
corresponding adjectives (explained on page 30). Note the accent
on all the forms except for the neuter – this is used to distinguish
these words from the demonstrative adjectives:

este almacén y **aquél** *this store and that one*
esa cuchara y **ésta** *that spoon and this one*

The neuter forms are only used to refer to ideas, statements, etc.
and never to specified nouns:

| ¿Has visto **esto**? | *Have you seen this?* |
| **esto** de los cheques | *this business about the cheques* |

Aquél can also translate *the former*, and **éste** *the latter*:

| Estaban hablando con Carmen y | *They were talking to Carmen and* |
| Rocío, y **éste** les dijo . . . | *Rocio, and the latter said to them. . .* |

▼ Activity 4   *Demonstrative pronouns*

Complete the following sentences with the appropriate demonstrative pronoun:

a ¿Qué sillas te gustan?
   (These) son más cómodas que *(those)*, pero las que me gustan más son *(those over there)*.

b ¿Qué piensas de estas novelas?
   (This one) es más interesante que *(that one)*, pero *(that one over there)* es muy aburrida.

c *(This)* será muy fácil, pero *(that)* será más difícil.

▼ Indefinite adjectives and pronouns

▼ *Algo, alguien, alguno*

Algo *something, anything*

| ¿Buscas **algo**? | *Are you looking for anything?* |
| **Algo** ha ocurrido. | *Something has happened.* |

In front of an adjective or adverb it can mean *somewhat, a little*:

| Está **algo** enojada. | *She is a little annoyed.* |

Algo de *a little* (quantity):

| Sabe **algo de** francés. | *He knows a little French.* |

Alguien *someone, anyone*

| Hay **alguien** en el vestíbulo. | *There is someone in the hall.* |

As an object it may be preceded by personal **a** (see page 58):

| Encontramos **a** alguien en la calle. | *We met someone in the street.* |

Alguno *some, a few*

It agrees like other adjectives, and drops the **o** before a masculine singular noun just like **uno** and **primero**, etc. (see pages 136 and 137) to become **algún** (always with an accent to show that it is stressed on the last syllable):

Ha vendido **algunos** periódicos.	*He has sold some newspapers.*
La carta llegará **algún** día.	*The letter will arrive some day.*

Unlike English, none of the above may be used after a negative. The appropriate negative is used instead:

No pueden ofrecer **nada**.	*They cannot offer anything.*
(See page 68.)	

▼ *Mucho, poco, tanto, todo*

These agree when used as adjectives or pronouns, but are invariable as adverbs:

Mucho *much, many;* poco *little, few*

Corremos **mucho**.	*We run a lot. (adverb)*
Construye **muchos** puentes.	*He builds many bridges. (adjective)*
Duerme **poco**.	*She sleeps little. (adverb)*
Plantan **pocos** pinos.	*They are planting few pine trees. (adjective)*

Tanto *so much, so many*

Las sandías tienen **tantas** pepitas.	*Watermelons have so many pips.*
Bebe **tanto**.	*He drinks so much.*

Todo *all, every, whole*

Todo está listo.	*Everything is ready.*
Todos se acostaron temprano.	*Everyone went to bed early.*

As an adjective it must always be accompanied by the definite article, a demonstrative or possessive adjective, or an object pronoun:

Ha estado aquí **toda la** semana.	*He has been here all week.*
Voy a revelar **todas mis** fotos.	*I am going to get all my photos developed.*
Hemos recibido **todo lo que** pedimos.	*We have received all we ordered.*
¿**Lo** apuntaste **todo**?	*Did you jot it all down?*

Exceptions:

when it means *each, every, any* in the singular:

Todo pasajero que lleva pasaporte español puede pasar por aquí.	*Any passenger with a Spanish passport can go through this way.*

or in the following expressions:

a/por todas partes	*everywhere*	de todos modos	*anyway*
a todos lados	*on all sides*		

del todo translates *completely*:

Está **del todo** lleno.	*It is completely full.*

todo el mundo (*everybody*) takes a singular verb:

Todo el mundo **está** feliz.	*Everybody is happy.*

▼ Activity 5 — *Indefinite adjectives and pronouns*

Complete these sentences inserting the appropriate expression from the following list:

todo lo, tanta, alguien, poco, del todo, muchas, algunos, algo, todo el mundo, todo

a . . . te ha llamado por teléfono.
b Hay . . . gente en la playa hoy.
c ¿Has probado . . . de estos licores?
d Parece que . . . ha visto esta película.
e Nos estaba contando . . . muy divertido.
f . . . familias ya tienen su propio ordenador.
g El juguete estaba . . . roto.
h Está contenta porque . . . está en orden.
i . . . que dice es mentiras.

▼ Other indefinite adjectives and pronouns

Varios/-as *several, various*

Encendieron **varias** luces.	*They switched on several lights.*
Varios de los plátanos están maduros.	*Several of the bananas are ripe.*

Cualquiera, cualesquiera (plural) *some, any* (vague)

It drops the **a** before a singular noun, either masculine or feminine:

Podría llegar a **cualquier** hora. *He could arrive at any time.*
Puedes llevar **cualquiera** de los *You can take any CD you like.*
discos compactos.

Los/las demás *the others, the remainder; the other, the remaining*; lo demás *the rest* (not referring to a specific noun)

Algunas de las botellas están en el *Some of the bottles are in the dining*
comedor, pero no sabemos dónde *room, but we do not know where*
están **las demás**. *the rest are.*
Esta parte es fácil, **lo demás** es *This part is easy, the rest is quite*
bastante difícil. *difficult.*

Otro *other, another (one[s])*

It is never preceded by an indefinite article:

estas camisas y **las otras** *these shirts and the other ones*
Están cargando **otra** camioneta. *They are loading up another van.*

Tal(es) *such, such a*

No indefinite article may be used after **tal**:

No escribirá **tal** cosa. *He will not write such a thing.*

Cada (invariable) *each, every*

As a pronoun it must be followed by **uno(a)**:

¿Cuánto cuesta **cada uno**? *How much are they each?*
Cada avenida parece igual. *Each avenue seems the same.*
Hace frío **cada** invierno. *It gets cold every winter.*

La mayoría de *most of* (individual units); la mayor parte de *most of* (a single unit)

La mayoría de los niños lo saben. *Most of the children know it.*
Se celebró **la mayor parte de** la *Most of the party was held in the*
fiesta al aire libre. *open air.*

Cierto *certain, a certain* (before the noun); *definite* (after the noun)

In the first meaning it is never preceded by an indefinite article:

Cierto vecino avisó a la policía.	*A certain neighbour notified the police.*
Ha sido un éxito **cierto**.	*It has been a definite success.*

Mismo *same* (before a noun); *-self*, etc. (after a noun or pronoun)

Siempre hace la **misma** pregunta.	*He always asks the same question.*
Lo tienes que conducir tú **mismo**.	*You must drive it yourself.*

As is translated by **que**:

Estos colores son los **mismos** **que** los otros.	*These colours are the same as the others.*

Note:

Mismo is also used after adverbs of time and place for emphasis:

Dejó el cuchillo aquí **mismo**.	*She left the knife right here.*
Va a comprar la radio ahora **mismo**.	*He is going to buy the radio right now.*

Ambos/(Ambos/-as); los/las dos *both*

Ambos is found mainly in written Spanish while **los/las dos** is used in spoken Spanish:

Las dos azafatas son guapas.	*Both air hostesses are pretty.*
Ambos datan del siglo XVIII.	*Both date from the 18th century.*

▼ *Linking indefinite adjectives and pronouns to the infinitive using* que

Tienes **alguna** ropa **que** lavar.	*You have some clothes to be washed.*
Encontró **algo que** comentar.	*He found something to discuss.*
No había **mucho que** organizar.	*There was not much to be organised.*
Tengo **cierta** idea **que** proponerte.	*I have a certain idea to put to you.*

▼▼▼
PREPOSITIONS
position and relation of things

As in English, prepositions are often required as link words after verbs, adjectives and nouns. For instance:

rico **en** hierro   *rich **in** iron*
lleno **de** leche   *full **of** milk*

In Spanish, a preposition is always placed *before* the word to which it refers.

▼ A guide to prepositions used after verbs

▼ *Prepositions required before another verb*

a + infinitive

Verbs of beginning and certain related verbs:

comenzar a ⎫   aprender a   *to learn to*
empezar a ⎪   disponerse a   *to get ready to*
ponerse a ⎬ *to begin to*   ayudar a   *to help to*
echarse a ⎭   forzar a   *to force to*
apresurarse a   *to hurry to*

Ella ayudó a su abuelo **a** incorporarse en la cama.   *She helped her grandfather sit up in bed.*

Verbs of motion when expressing purpose:

Salen **a** comer.   *They are going out to eat.*
Vino **a** felicitarte.   *He came to congratulate you.*

Certain verbs of repetition:

volver a   *to do something again*

de + infinitive

Verbs of finishing:

terminar de ⎤
cesar de ⎬ to finish
dejar de ⎦
acabar de   to have just (done something)

Terminan **de** trabajar a las seis.   *They stop working at six.*

por + infinitive

Verbs of beginning/finishing by:

empezar, etc. por   *to begin by*   terminar, etc. por   *to finish by*

La orquesta empezó el concierto **por**   *The orchestra began the concert by*
tocar un vals.   *playing a waltz.*

The following types require no preposition before an infinitive:

Verbs of influence, such as those of advising, making, ordering, wanting, preventing, permitting, needing:

aconsejar	*to advise*	preferir	*to prefer*
hacer	*to make*	impedir	*to prevent*
mandar	*to order*	permitir	*to allow*
querer	*to want*	necesitar	*to need*

Quiero comprar unas postales.   *I want to buy some postcards.*

Verbs of the senses:

ver   *to see*   oír   *to hear*   sentir   *to feel*

Vimos nadar a Juan.   *We saw Juan swim.*

Verbs which behave like **gustar** (see page 122) and other impersonal verbs:

No le gusta ir de compras con su   *He doesn't like going shopping with*
hermana.   *his sister.*

▼ Prepositions required before either another verb or an object

de

Verbs describing emotions:

alegrarse de	*to be glad about*
avergonzarse de	*to be ashamed of*
gozar de	*to enjoy*
enamorarse de	*to fall in love with*
hartarse de	*to be/get fed up with*
preocuparse de	*to worry about*

Su hija se ha enamorado **de** un joven policía.	*His daughter has fallen in love with a young policeman.*

Also:

abstenerse de	*to abstain/refrain from*
prescindir de	*to do without*
olvidarse de	*to forget (but no preposition after* **olvidar**)
carecer de	*to lack*

Se ha olvidado **de** traer las llaves.	*He has forgotten to bring the keys.*

▼ Prepositions required before an object

a

Verbs of approaching:

acercarse a ⎫	*to approach*
aproximarse a ⎬	
arrimarse a	*to lean against*

¿Todavía no se han sentado **a** la mesa?	*Haven't they sat down at the table yet?*

Verbs describing resemblance or comparison:

parecerse a	*to resemble*
comparar a	*to compare with*
saber a	*to taste of*
oler a	*to smell of*

La sopa huele **a** ajo.	*The soup smells of garlic.*

de

Verbs describing separation:

alejarse de ⎫ apartarse de ⎭	to move away from
despedirse de	to say goodbye to
mudarse de	to move (house), change

Los niños se despidieron **de** sus amigos desde el balcón.

The children said goodbye to their friends from the balcony.

Verbs describing filling, covering, etc. with:

cargar de	to load with
llenar de	to fill with
cubrir de	to cover with

El camión estaba cargado **de** heno.

The lorry was laden with hay.

Common verbs that require a preposition in English but not in Spanish

aguardar ⎫ esperar ⎭	to wait for
escuchar	to listen to
pedir	to ask for
aprovechar	to profit from, take advantage of
buscar	to look for
tirar	to throw away

Los turistas están esperando el autobús.

The tourists are waiting for the bus.

▼ A list of common verbs showing what preposition, if any, they take before another

aburrirse de *to get bored with*
acabar con *to put an end to*
acabar de *to have just*
acabar por *to finish by*
aconsejar *to advise*
acordarse con *to agree with*
acordarse de *to remember,*
  to agree to

acostumbrarse a
  to get accustomed to
advertir de *to notify, warn*
aguardar a *to wait until*
alegrarse de *to be glad*
alejarse de *to move away from*
aprender a *to learn to*
aprobar *to approve of*

asistir a *to be present at*

asombrarse de *to be surprised at*

asustarse de *to be frightened at*

ayudar a *to help to*

bajar de *to get off/out of (vehicles)*

burlarse de *to make fun of*

cansarse de *to tire of*

casar a *to marry off*

casarse con *to get married to*

cesar de *to stop (doing)*

comentar *to comment on, discuss*

comenzar a *to begin to*

comparar a *to compare to*

comparar con *to compare with*

conducir a *to lead to*

consentir en *to agree to*

consistir en *to consist of*

contar con *to rely, count on*

contestar a *to reply to*

convenir a *to suit (people)*

convenir con *to agree with*

convenir en *to agree to*

convidar a *to invite to*

creer *to believe*

dar a *to look onto* (e.g. window)

dar con *to run across*

darse cuenta de *to realise*

deber *must, to have to*

deber de *must, to have to*

decidir *to decide*

dejar *to allow, let*

dejar de *to stop (doing)*

depender de *to depend on*

desear *to desire to*

despedirse de *to say goodbye to*

empezar a *to begin to*

empezar por *to begin by*

enamorarse de *to fall in love with*

encontrarse con *to meet*

enseñar a *to teach how to*

entrar en *to enter*

escuchar *to listen to*

esperar a *to wait until*

estar de acuerdo con *to agree with*

examinarse en *to take an exam in*

haber de *to have to*

hablar con *to talk to*

hacer daño a *to harm*

intentar *to try to*

interesarse en *to be interested in*

invitar a *to invite to*

jugar a *to play*

lograr *to succeed in, manage to*

llegar a *to reach*

mandar *to order to*

mirar *to look at*

mirar a *to look towards*

necesitar *to need*

ocuparse de *to take care of,*
    attend to

ofrecer *to offer to*

oler a *to smell of*

olvidar *to forget*

olvidarse de *to forget*

parecer *to seem*

parecerse a *to resemble*

pedir *to ask for (things)*

pensar en/de *to think about/of*

permitir *to allow to*

persuadir a *to persuade to*

poder *to be able to*

ponerse a *to start to*

preferir *to prefer*

preguntar por *to ask for (people)*

preocuparse de/por *to worry about*

prepararse a *to prepare to*

quedar en *to agree to*

quedar por *to remain to be (done)*

quedarse a *to remain/stay to*

quejarse de *to complain of*

recordar *to remember*

reírse de *to laugh at*

resistir a *to resist*

rogar *to request*

saber *to know how to*

saber a *to taste of*

salir de *to leave*

sentarse a *to sit down to/at*

sentir *to feel, sense, regret*
servir de *to serve as*
servir para *to be good for*
servirse de *to use*
sonreírse de *to smile at*
sorprenderse de *to be surprised at*
subir(se) a *to get on/into (vehicles)*
tardar en *to take a long time, be slow (doing)*
tener ganas de *to want to*
tener miedo a *to be afraid of (people)*

tener miedo de *to be afraid of (things)*
tener que *to have to*
terminar por *to end by*
trabajar de *to work as*
trabajar en *to work at*
trabajar por/para *to work to/for*
tratar de *to try to*
tratarse de *to be a question of*
vestirse de *to be dressed as*
volver a *to return to; do again*

▼ Prepositions after adjectives and nouns

Where an infinitive is the subject of a verb, no preposition is used before it:

Escuchar música es muy agradable.
Listening to music is very pleasant.

Leer es imposible con este ruido.
Reading is impossible with this noise.

Otherwise a preposition is always used. The most common is **de**:

Esta novela es difícil **de** leer.
This novel is difficult to read.

Gonzalo es capaz **de** ser muy eficaz.
Gonzalo is capable of being very efficient.

¿Me hace el favor **de** firmar aquí?
Could you please sign here?

The preposition used is often the same as that following a related verb, for example:

parecido a	*similar to*	(parecerse a)
dispuesto a	*ready to*	(disponerse a)
rodeado de	*surrounded by*	(rodear de)
obligado a	*obliged to*	(obligar a)
la lucha por	*the struggle to*	(luchar por)

Note also:

de
after superlatives:

Es la mejor habitación **del** hotel.
It is the best room in the hotel.

con
attitude towards:

Está furiosa **con** ellos.
She is furious with them.

Estaba severo **con** sus estudiantes.
He was strict with his students.

en
ability in something:

Eres bueno/fuerte **en** matemáticas.	*You are good at maths.*
Es malo **en** biología.	*He is bad at biology.*

between **primero**, **último** and **único** and infinitive:

Fue el primero/último/único **en** llegar.	*He was the first/last/only one to arrive.*

▼ Using prepositions

This section gives a list of all the common prepositions with their literal meanings and some of the most important idiomatic expressions in which they are used.

▼ A
General uses
to, onto

a ti	*to you*
a Madrid	*to Madrid*
a la izquierda	*to/on the left*
Cayó **al** suelo.	*It fell onto the floor.*
Pegó el sello **al** sobre.	*He stuck the stamp onto the envelope.*
Ella añadirá leche **al** café.	*She will add milk to the coffee.*

at (time)

a la una	*at one*
a los trece años	*at the age of thirteen*
a veces	*at times*
a fines del año	*at the end of the year*
a tiempo	*on time*
al día siguiente	*the next day*

at/by (next to/distance but not *in*)

a la puerta	*at the door*
a orillas del mar	*by the seaside*
a 10 km de aquí	*10 km from here*

at (rate)

a 50 k.p.h.	*at 50 k.p.h.*
tres veces **al** mes	*three times a month*

at (price)

a 200 ptas. el kilo	*at 200 pesetas a kilo*

in (weather, etc.)

al sol	*in the sun*
al viento	*in the wind*
a la sombra	*in the shade*

but:

bajo la lluvia	*in the rain*

from people (after verbs of removal, purchase, hiding, etc.)

Le robaron £500 **al** sastre.	*They stole £500 from the tailor.*
¿**A** quién compraste la bicicleta?	*From whom did you buy the bicycle?*
El chico escondió el juguete **a** su hermano.	*The boy hid the toy from his brother.*

before objects of verbs of the senses used together with another verb:

Vemos **al** pájaro volar en el cielo.	*We can see the bird flying in the sky.*

in certain expressions, such as:

a mi ver	*in my opinion*	a caballo	*on horseback*
a lo lejos	*in the distance*	al contrario	*on the contrary*
al teléfono	*on the telephone*	poco a poco	*little by little*
a pie	*on foot*		

Al + infinitive *on/while* (doing something), etc.

Al llegar al aeropuerto, alquilamos un coche.	*On arriving at the airport, we hired a car.*

Personal 'a'
Whenever a specific person or domestic animal is the direct object of a verb, the so-called personal **a** is placed in front of it:

La bala hirió **al** soldado.	The bullet wounded the soldier.
La chica echa de menos **a** su caballo.	The girl misses her horse.

but:

Buscamos una cocinera.	We are looking for a cook. (any cook)
Detesta los abogados.	He hates lawyers. (all lawyers)

▼ Antes de, delante de, ante
Antes de *before(time)*

antes de la una	before one o'clock
antes de viernes	before Friday

Delante de *before (in front of)*

Estaban de pie **delante de** la puerta.	They were standing in front of the door.

Ante *before (in the presence of, faced with)*

Comparecerá **ante** el juez.	He will appear before the judge.
No se puede hacer nada **ante** esa situación.	One cannot do anything when faced with that situation.

▼ De
of

los guantes **de** la vieja	the old woman's gloves

(The 's construction does not exist in Spanish.)

una botella **de** coñac	a bottle of brandy
tres **de** los gatos	three of the cats

in many other adjectival phrases:

un collar **de** perlas	a pearl necklace
el avión **de** Quito	the Quito plane
el hijo **de** ocho años	the eight-year-old son
un edificio **de** diez pisos	a ten-storey building

miscellaneous expressions:

de acuerdo	O.K.		de veras	really
de prisa	in a hurry		de pie	standing
de moda	in fashion		ir de compras	to go shopping
de repente	suddenly			

from (see also **a** above and **desde** below)

el turista **de** Italia	*the tourist from Italy*
Llegaron **de** la ciudad.	*They arrived from the town.*
de vez en cuando	*from time to time*
Data **del** siglo XVI.	*It dates from the 16th century.*

of, about

Hablan **de** religión.	*They are talking about religion.*

▼ *Debajo de, bajo*
under, below

debajo de is used more frequently in the physical sense:

La cesta está { **debajo de** / **bajo** } la mesa.　*The basket is under the table.*

bajo is mainly used in figurative senses:

bajo el gobierno democrático	*under the democratic government*
dos grados **bajo** cero	*two degrees below zero/minus two*

▼ *Desde*
from a point (with verbs of seeing, calling, throwing, etc.)

Le llamaron **desde** el comedor.	*They called him from the dining room.*
Los chicos estaban tirando piedras **desde** el puente.	*The boys were throwing stones from the bridge.*
desde tu punto de vista	*from your point of view*

from (onwards)

Desde Granada el paisaje era más interesante.	*Fom Granada onwards the countryside was more interesting.*

desde . . . hasta: *from . . . to* (usually to emphasise distance or time)

desde las tres **hasta** las cinco	*from three to five o'clock*
Durmió en el tren **desde** Toledo **hasta** Cuenca.	*He slept on the train all the way from Toledo to Cuenca.*

since

desde ayer	*since yesterday*

▼ *En*

in (or *at*)

en el camión	*in the lorry*	**en** 1900	*in 1900*
en el hospital	*at/in the hospital*	**en** 15 minutos	*in 15 minutes*
en vano	*in vain*	**en** voz baja	*in a low voice*
en paz	*at/in peace*		

(but: llegar **a** *to arrive in;* salir **a** *to go out into)*

For expressions of weather, see page 58.

into

Entra **en** el vestíbulo.	*He goes into the hall.*
Metí la mano **en** el bolsillo.	*I put my hand in(to) my pocket.*

by (transport)

en avión	*by plane*
en autobús	*by bus*
(See also **a** and **por** on pages 57, 63.)	

at (time – occasionally)

en este momento	*at this moment*
en aquella época	*at that time*

on (place)

en la mesa	*on the table*
en el suelo	*on the ground*
en el tercer piso	*on the third floor*

To avoid any confusion in the use of **en** (*on* or *in*), **encima de** (*on top of, above*) or **sobre** (*on, above*) can be used instead:

Los platos están **encima del** horno.	*The plates are on top of the stove.*
La ropa está **sobre** la cama.	*The clothes are on the bed.*

Miscellaneous expressions:

en cuanto	*as soon as*
en seguida	*immediately*
en cambio	*on the other hand*
lavar en seco	*to dry clean*

▼ *Hacia*
towards

El sereno se dirige **hacia** la puerta.

The night watchman is heading for the door.

Hacia may be combined with the following to convey motion in a particular direction: **arriba** (*above*), **abajo** (*below*), **adelante** (*forward*), **atrás** (*back*), **adentro** (*inside*), **afuera** (*outside*), for example:

hacia arriba   *upwards*
hacia atrás   *backwards*

hacia afuera   *outwards*
hacia adentro   *inwards*

around (time)

hacia las once
(*alternatively:* **a eso de . . ., sobre . . .**)

at around eleven

▼ *Hasta*
until, up to (time)

hasta julio
hasta ahora

until July
up to now

as far as

Siga **hasta** el semáforo.

Go straight on as far as the traffic lights.

up to (numerically)

Conté **hasta** sesenta personas.

I counted up to sixty people.

even, including

Hasta ellos se asombraron.

Even they were surprised.

▼ *Para*
for (purpose, destination, use, suitability)

la llave **para** el coche
un regalo **para** su novia
Sale **para** Venezuela.
¿**Para** qué necesitas tanto dinero?

the key for the car
a present for his girlfriend
He is leaving for Venezuela.
What do you need so much money for?

apto **para** el empleo	*suitable for the job*
útil **para** el jardín	*useful for the garden*
Es muy malo **para** la salud.	*It is very bad for one's health.*

by, for a future moment

| Se fijó la reunión **para** el día diez. | *The party was arranged for the tenth.* |
| **Para** cuando regreses ya estará listo. | *By the time you return it will be ready.* |

for (bearing in mind, considering, etc.)

| Hace mucho frío **para** mayo. | *It is very cold for May.* |
| Es muy grande **para** sus años. | *He is very tall for his age.* |

Miscellaneous expressions:

para siempre	*for ever*
para empezar	*to start with*
leer para sí	*to read to oneself*

▼ *Por*

along, through, around, about (motion)

Anduvimos **por** el sendero.	*We walked along the path.*
Pase **por** aquí.	*Come along here./Step this way.*
El tren pasa **por** el túnel.	*The train goes through the tunnel.*
Lanzó un ladrillo **por** la ventana.	*He threw a brick through the window.*
Viajarán **por** Francia.	*They will travel through France.*
Vaga **por** la cuidad.	*He is wandering around the town.*

Por is also combined with the following to convey motion:

encima de	*on top of, above*	**por** encima de	*over*
debajo de	*under*	**por** debajo de	*under*
delante de	*in front of*	**por** delante de	*past*
detrás de	*behind*	**por** detrás de	*behind*
entre	*between, among*	**por** entre	*through, between*
donde	*where*	**por** donde	*the way that, along which, by way of which*
¿dónde?	*where?*	¿**por** dónde?	*which way*

| El buzón está delante de la farmacia. | *The letter box is in front of the chemist's.* |
| El joven corrió **por delante de la** puerta de la panadería. | *The lad ran past the bakery door.* |

Los libros están debajo del escritorio.	*The books are under the desk.*
El coche va a pasar **por debajo del** puente.	*The car is going to go under the bridge.*

in, around, about, etc. (vague location)

Había polvo **por** todas partes.	*There was dust everywhere.*
¿Hay un hotel **por** aquí?	*Is there a hotel near here?*

in, around, etc. (time – usually vague)

por la mañana	*in the morning*
por aquel entonces	*at around that time*
por Navidad	*at Christmas time*

(It is not used with time of the clock – see **hacia** on page 62.)

by, per, etc. (rate)

100 km **por** hora	*100 km per hour*
un veinte **por** ciento	*twenty per cent*
cinco veces **por** hora	*five times an hour*

by (with the passive – see pages 111–13)

Las drogas fueron descubiertas **por** el aduanero.	*The drugs were discovered by the customs officer.*

by (means of)

por correo aéreo	*by airmail*
llamar **por** teléfono	*to telephone*
por barco	*by boat*

(In Spain **por** is normally used for freight, **en** for passengers.)

for, because, etc. (cause, reason)

por eso	*for that reason*
¿**por** qué?	*why, for what reason?*
Han ido **por** leche.	*They have gone to get some milk.*
No viene **por** estar enferma.	*She is not coming because she is ill.*
por lo que dicen	*judging by what they say*

for (exchange)

Mi hermano me dio 2000 ptas. **por** el disco compacto.	*My brother gave me 2000 pesetas for the CD.*

but **por** is omitted if no price is mentioned:

Pagaba la comida.   *He was paying for the meal.*

for (considered equivalence)

por ejemplo   *for example*
Les dejaron **por** muertos.   *They left them for dead.*

for (feelings)

No siente nada **por** ellos.   *He feels nothing for them.*

however + adjective or adverb

por muchos que haya   *however many there may be*

to, to be + infinitive (action to be completed)

cuentas **por** pagar   *bills to be paid*

(See also page 50.)

for (for the sake of, in favour of, for the benefit of, on behalf of, instead of)

por amor de Dios   *for the love of God*
Lo haremos **por** ti.   *We will do it for you.*

Numerous miscellaneous expressions including:

por fin	*finally, at last*	por una parte	*on the one hand*
por lo menos	*at least*	por desgracia	*unfortunately*
por casualidad	*by chance*	por supuesto	*of course*
por completo	*completely*	por lo visto	*apparently*
por escrito	*in writing*	por mí	*as far as I'm concerned*

▼ *Según*
according to

Según la radio va a llover mañana.   *According to the radio it will rain tomorrow.*

as (progression)

Según avanzábamos nos sentíamos cada vez más cansados.   *As we walked on we felt more and more tired.*

as, just as

El cuarto está **según** lo dejó. | *The room is just as he left it.*

▼ *Sobre*
on (place – see also **en** on page 61)

Las cucharas están **sobre** la mesa. | *The spoons are on the table.*
El mural **sobre** esa pared es de Diego Rivera. | *The mural on that wall is by Diego Rivera.*

on, about (concerning)

Hay una conferencia **sobre** Fidel Castro a las dos. | *There is a lecture on Fidel Castro at two.*

above, over

El avión voló **sobre** el mar. | *The plane flew over the sea.*
quince grados **sobre** cero | *five degrees above zero*

about (approximately)

Santiago tiene **sobre** cuatro millones de habitantes. | *Santiago has about four million inhabitants.*
La película empieza **sobre** las siete y media. | *The film starts at about half past seven.*

▼ General observations

- Spanish prepositions must always come before the word to which they refer:

la señora **con** quien habla | *the lady he is talking with*
¿**De** qué se trata? | *What is it about?*

- Any prepositions required after verbs and nouns, etc. are usually retained when followed by another clause:

Aguarda **a** que venga. | *Wait until he comes.*
Nos alegramos **de** que se haya casado. | *We are glad he has got married.*
Tiene miedo **de** que suceda otra vez. | *He is afraid of it happening again.*

NEGATIVES, QUESTIONS, EXCLAMATIONS

▼ Negative forms

▼ *Simple negatives*

The simplest way to make a statement negative is by adding **no** between the subject and the verb:

| La puerta es azul. | *The door is blue.* |
| La puerta **no** es azul. | *The door is not blue.* |

No is placed in front of any object pronouns that precede the verb (see page 38):

| Yo se lo enviaré. | *I will send it to him.* |
| Yo **no** se lo enviaré. | *I will not send it to him.* |

In phrases like *not me, not today,* etc., the Spanish **no** usually comes after the word or phrase to which it belongs:

yo **no**	*not me*
hoy **no**	*not today*
el que está allí **no**, el otro	*not the one that is over there, the other one*

When *not* forms a kind of object of verbs of saying, hoping, thinking, etc., it is translated by **que no**:

Esperas **que no**.	*You hope not.*
Creemos **que no**.	*We don't think so.*
Supongo **que no**.	*I suppose not.*

Note also:

| claro **que no** | *of course not* |

The positive form is **que sí**:

Esperas **que sí**.	*You hope so.*
claro **que sí**	*of course (yes)*
Supongo **que sí**.	*I suppose so.*

▼ Double negatives

no . . . nada	nothing, not anything	no . . . tampoco	not . . . either
no . . . nadie	nobody, not anybody	no . . . ni . . . ni	neither . . . nor
no . . . nunca	never, not ever	no . . . ni siquiera	not even
no . . . jamás	never (stronger)	no . . . más	no longer, not
no . . . ninguno	no (adjective), not any		any longer
		no . . . más que	only

* When any of the above appear after a verb, **no** must go before the verb:

Ellos **no** escogieron **nada**.	They did not choose anything.
No nieva **nunca** allí.	It never snows there.
No lo sabe ella **tampoco**.	She does not know either.
Eso **no** le interesa **más**.	That does not interest him any longer.
No nos quedan **más que** 100 pesos.	We have only 100 pesos left.

* **Ninguno** agrees, but drops the **o** in front of masculine singular nouns, adding an accent to show the stress. It should not be used in the plural:

¿No oyes **ningún** pájaro?	Can't you hear any birds?
No va a llamar a **ninguno** de los clientes.	He is not going to call any of the clients.
No tenemos **ninguna** mañana libre.	We have no free mornings.

* There are three degrees or levels of negation:

No tiene dinero.	He has no money.
No tiene **ningún** dinero.	He hasn't got any money.
No tiene dinero **alguno**.	He hasn't got any money at all.

* **Nadie** and **ni . . . ni** may be used with personal **a** (see page 57):

No espero a **nadie**.	I am not waiting for anyone.
No conocéis **ni** a Pablo **ni** a Esteban.	You don't know either Pablo or Esteban.

* **Nada** means *not at all* when it refers to an adjective or adverb:

La estatua no es **nada** impresionante.	The statue is not at all impressive.

- **Nadie, nada** and **ninguno** are linked to an infinitive by **que**:

No tengo **nada que** leer.	*I have nothing to read.*
No había **nadie que** preguntar.	*There was nobody to ask.*
No tenía **ninguna** comida **que** preparar.	*She had no meal to prepare.*

- **Jamás** used after the verb but not preceded by **no** just means *ever*:

¿**No** visita **jamás** a su tía?	*Does he never visit his aunt?/Doesn't he ever visit his aunt?*
¿Visita **jamás** a su tía?	*Does he ever visit his aunt?*

- Two negatives may be used together as follows:

La vieja no ve **nunca** a **nadie**.	*The old woman never sees anyone.*
La tienda no vende **nunca nada** barato.	*The shop never sells anything cheap.*

- Two interdependent verbs may never be split by a negative:

No **ha conducido** nunca un coche.	*He has never driven a car.*
No **pueden recordar** nada.	*They cannot remember anything.*
No **está cenando** más.	*He is no longer having supper.*

▼ Use of negatives before a verb

With the exception of **más** and **más que**, the negatives above may be placed before the verb. **No** is no longer used with them:

Nadie lo confirmó.	*Nobody confirmed it.*
Tú **nunca** olvidarás ese accidente.	*You will never forget that accident.*
Ni esta casa **ni** la otra está en venta.	*Neither this house nor the other one is for sale.*

Ni used on its own can also mean *not even, not a single*:

El **ni** había empezado su trabajo.	*He had not even begun his work.*
No había **ni** un barco.	*There was not a single boat.*

▼ Activity 1 *Negatives*

Make the following sentences negative:

a Alguien estaba mirando la televisión.
b Le gusta alguna de estas corbatas.
c Este coche o el otro es el más caro.
d ¿Siempre trabajáis en el jardín los fines de semana?
e Han vendido el cuadro también.

▼ *Negatives in short replies*

Practically all these negatives may be used without a verb in a short statement:

¿Quién está allí? **Nadie.**	*Who is there? Nobody.*
¿Cuántas veces has esquiado? **Nunca.**	*How many times have you skied? Never.*
El no está de acuerdo. Yo **tampoco**.	*He does not agree. Nor do I.*

▼ *Negatives in comparisons*

The negatives must be used in the following type of comparison:

Estás jugando mejor que **nunca**.	*You are playing better than ever.*
Más que **nada** les gustaría vivir en el campo.	*More than anything they would like to live in the country.*

▼ *Other negatives*

- **Todavía/Aún . . . no** *still . . . not*: **no . . . todavía/aún** *not . . . yet*

Aún no se atreve a saltar.	*He still does not dare jump.*
¿Se ha despertado? No, **todavía no**.	*Has he woken up? No, not yet.*

- **Sin** *without*

Salió **sin** su sombrero.	*He went out without his hat.*

Sin must always be followed by a negative (English uses a positive):

Se fueron **sin** ver a **nadie**.	*They left without seeing anyone.*

As with double negatives above, there are three degrees of negation:

Lo haremos **sin** problema.	*We will do it without a problem.*
Lo haremos **sin ningún** problema.	*We will do it without any problem.*
Lo haremos **sin** problema alguno.	*We will do it without the slightest problem.*

- **Sin que** is used before a finite verb (i.e. not an infinitive) and takes the subjunctive (see pages 92–3):

Lo empezaron **sin que** nos diésemos cuenta.	*They began it without our realising it.*

- **Sino** translates *but* after a negative where the first statement is clearly contradicted:

No busca el ayuntamiento **sino** la comisaría.	*He is not looking for the town hall but the police station.*
No viajaremos en tren **sino** en avión.	*We won't travel by train but by plane.*

but

Yo no fumo, **pero** no me molesta si Vd. quiere fumar.	*I don't smoke, but I don't mind if you want to smoke.*

Sino can also mean *but* in the sense of *except*:

No te lo puede decir nadie **sino** ella.	*Nobody can tell you but her.*

- **Sino que** is used before a finite verb:

El pueblo no sólo tiene un hotel de primera clase, **sino que** también tiene unos restaurantes excelentes.	*The town not only has a first class hotel, but it also has some excellent restaurants.*

▼ Question forms (interrogatives)

Question words, or 'interrogatives', always have an accent in Spanish, to distinguish them from their non-question equivalents.

- ¿Qué? ¿Cuál? *Which? What?*

In Spanish **qué** is used to translate *which* or *what* as an adjective (with the noun immediately after it):

¿**Qué** disco compacto vas a comprar?	*Which CD are you going to buy?*
¿**Qué** platos les gustan más?	*What dishes do they like most?*

Qué and **cuál** are both used as pronouns (standing alone), each in different circumstances.

Qué is used to ask for general information or a definition:

¿**Qué** os asustó?	*What frightened you?*
¿Con **qué** lo vamos a cubrir?	*What are we going to cover it with?*
¿**Qué** están sembrando?	*What are they sowing?*
¿**Qué** es Rodrigo? Es futbolista.	*What is Rodrigo? He's a footballer.*
¿**Qué** son los sueños?	*What are dreams?*

Cuál (*which?/what?*) is used to ask for more specific information, indicating a choice or a distinction between related people or objects, etc.:

¿**Cuál** es la capital de Colombia?	*What is the capital of Colombia?.*
¿**Cuál** es su apellido?	*What is your surname?*
¿**Cuál** es su opinión?	*What is your opinion?*
¿**Cuál** es la diferencia entre jerez y manzanilla?	*What is the difference between sherry and manzanilla?*
¿**Cuál** de estas carreteras es la mejor?	*Which of these roads is the best?*
¿**Cuáles** de estos zapatos prefiere?	*Which of these shoes does he prefer?*

- ¿Quién? *Who?*

¿Quién(es)?	*Who? (subject or after preposition)*
¿A quién(es)?	*Whom? (object)*
¿De quién(es)?	*Whose?*
¿**Quién** asistió a la boda? ⎫	*Who attended the wedding?*
¿**Quiénes** asistieron a la boda? ⎭	
¿**A quién** detuvieron?	*Whom did they arrest?*
¿**De quién** es este reloj?	*Whose is this watch?*

¿**De quién**? is never placed next to the noun like an adjective. **Cuyo** (see Relative Pronouns on pages 42–4) is never used in questions.

- *When, where, why, how?*

¿Cuándo?	*When?*	¿Cómo?	*How?*
¿Dónde?	*Where?*	¿Por qué?	*Why?*
¿Adónde?	*Where . . . to?*	¿Cuánto?	*How much/many? (it agrees when used adjectivally)*

¿**Cómo**? is also used in conversation when asking someone to repeat what they have just said:

– Su dirección es: Avenida Artigas 2036, primer piso, oficina no. 103.	*Her address is: Avenida Artigas 2036, first floor, office no. 103.*
– ¿**Cómo**?	*Sorry (could you say that again)?*

All the above interrogatives are used in indirect questions as well and have an accent:

No sabe **cuál** escogerá.	*He does not know which he will choose.*
El capitán se preguntó **por qué** habían perdido.	*The captain wondered why they had lost.*
Los detectives están investigando **cómo** entraron los ladrones.	*The detectives are investigating how the thieves got in.*

▼ Activity 2   *Forming questions*

Complete the sentences below using one of the following expressions,
some of which may be used more than once:
cuál, cuáles, de quién, quién, a quiénes, qué, cómo, cuándo.

a ¿. . . acompañó a tu tía?
b ¿. . . termina el programa?
c ¿. . . secretaria trabaja aquí?
d ¿. . . son estos mapas?
e ¿. . . es la calle donde vivieron?
f ¿. . . de estas bebidas prefieren Vds.?
g No sabemos en . . . hotel pasó la noche.
h Habíamos preguntado . . . habían invitado.
i Le está explicando . . . perdió sus llaves ayer.
j No sabe . . . escogerá de estas manzanas.

▼ Exclamations

Words introducing exclamations always have an accent in Spanish.

Quién, cuánto, cómo and **qué** may also be used in exclamations:

¡**Quién** lo hubiera creído!	*Who would have believed it!*
¡**Cuánto** pesa!	*How heavy it is!*
¡**Cómo**! ¿Ha subido otra vez el precio del pan?	*What! Has the price of bread gone up yet again?*

Qué in an exclamation translates:

- *what, what a* + noun

The English *a* is never translated. If, as is usually the case, the
adjective follows the noun, it is linked to it by **más** or **tan**:

¡**Qué** lástima!	*What a pity!*
¡**Qué** perro **tan/más** feroz!	*What a fierce dog!*

- *how* + adjective or adverb:

¡**Qué** ridículo!	*How ridiculous!*

VERBS
saying what is happening

Verbs are the action words in a sentence: they tell us what the subject is doing, what is happening to the object, etc.

▼ Groups of verbs

All verbs in Spanish are divided into three groups, or 'conjugations', according to their endings in the infinitive:

-AR	-ER	-IR
hablar *to speak*	comer *to eat*	vivir *to live*

These three verbs have been used through most of the regular verb section to illustrate the formation of the Spanish tenses. The English tenses have been illustrated by the first person singular (*I* form) or other relevant part of the verb *to speak*.

stem:

Unless otherwise stated, this means the infinitive without the final -**ar**, -**er** or -**ir**.

personal endings:

The order in which these are shown is as follows:

yo	*I*	(1st person singular)
tú	*you*	(2nd person singular)
él, ella, Vd.	*he, she, it, you*	(3rd person singular)
nosotros	*we*	(1st person plural)
vosotros	*you*	(2nd person plural)
ellos, ellas, Vds.	*they, you*	(3rd person plural)

(The different translations of *you* are explained on pages 8–9.)

Irregular verbs
Not all Spanish verbs follow exactly the patterns described below. Some have irregularities in a few tenses and several are very irregular. The common irregular verbs are listed on pages 147–59.

▼ Simple and compound tenses

When you are learning how to form the different tenses in Spanish, it is useful to divide them into **simple** and **compound** tenses.

In simple tenses the verb is just one word: e.g. trabajo *I am working/I work*, trabajaba *he was working/he worked*.

The simple tenses in Spanish are: present, future, conditional, imperfect, preterite.

In compound tenses, the verb has two parts: the part of **haber** (the auxiliary verb) and the past participle: e.g. he comido *I have eaten*, había visto *he had seen*.

The compound tenses in Spanish are: perfect, pluperfect, past anterior, future perfect, conditional perfect.

▼ The present tense

The present tense is used to describe actions which are taking place now or are habitual.

All of the following are examples of the present tense in English: *I speak, I do speak, I don't speak, do I speak?*

▼ *Forming the present tense*
stem + present endings:

hablo	como	vivo
hablas	comes	vives
habla	come	vive
hablamos	comemos	vivimos
habláis	coméis	vivís
hablan	comen	viven

▼ *Using the present tense*
The same as in English:

¿**Viven** en Madrid?	*Do they live in Madrid?*
Creo que **está** enfermo.	*I think he is ill.*

• but also for the immediate or planned future:

¡Ya **voy**!	*I am coming!*
Le **escribimos** mañana.	*We will write to him tomorrow.*

....

• as a polite command or request

¿Me **traes** la mantequilla, por favor?	*Could you fetch me the butter, please?*

• to translate *shall* in suggestions:

¿**Cierro** la puerta?	*Shall I shut the door?*
¿Nos **sentamos** aquí?	*Shall we sit down here?*

• to convey actions more vividly in a narrative (a usage known as the 'historic present'):

En 1881 **nace** Picasso en Málaga.	*In 1881 Picasso was born in Málaga.*

• to describe an action or state begun in the past and continuing into the present:

Está en casa desde las tres.	*He has been at home since three.*

(This is an important difference between Spanish and English and it is explained more fully on pages 126–7.)

The English form *I do speak* is often used for emphasis. To translate this into Spanish put **sí** before the verb:

No habla francés, pero **sí** habla español.	*He doesn't speak French, but he does speak Spanish.*

▼ Activity 1   *The present tense*

Put the verbs in brackets into the correct form of the present tense:

a ¿Qué deportes (practicar) vosotros?
Yo (nadar), Marta (patinar), y Roberto y Julio (pescar). Roberto y yo (montar) a caballo también. Y tú ¿qué deportes (practicar)?

b ¿Qué (beber) vosotros generalmente?
Yo (beber) cerveza, mis hermanos menores (beber) Coca Cola y mi hermana mayor (beber) café. Y tú ¿qué (beber)?

c ¿A quiénes (escribir) vosotros?
Yo (escribir) a mi hija, Arturo (escribir) a su esposa y ellas (escribir) a su primo. Y tú ¿a quién (escribir)?

▼ The imperfect tense

This tense describes actions which used to happen or were happening in the past.

The Spanish imperfect tense translates the English forms *I was speaking, I used to speak.*

▼ *Forming the imperfect*

Stem + imperfect endings:

hablaba	comía	vivía
hablabas	comías	vivías
hablaba	comía	vivía
hablábamos	comíamos	vivíamos
hablabais	comíais	vivíais
hablaban	comían	vivían

▼ *Using the imperfect*

Although both English forms are translated by the Spanish imperfect, the first may also be translated by the imperfect continuous (see pages 100–1) if you want to emphasise the fact that an action was going on at a precise moment in the past, as in the second example below.

El sol **brillaba** y el cielo **era** de un azul claro.

The sun was shining and the sky was bright blue.

Cuando entré, mi hermana **estaba mirando** la televisión.

When I went in, my sister was watching the television.

The Spanish imperfect is also used to translate the English simple past (*I spoke*, etc.) in the following cases:

* to describe habitual actions when it translates the English *used to* or *would* (*do something*):

En verano se **levantaba** muy temprano cada día.

In the summer he got up/would get up/used to get up early every day.

* to describe settings or situations in the past:

Cuando los gemelos **tenían** 16 años, su padre murió.

When the twins were 16, their father died.

* including time:

Eran las cinco.

It was five o'clock.

- generally when using verbs of wanting, thinking, knowing, fearing, being able, etc. to describe mental activity or a state of mind in the past:

Quería saber dónde está el cine. — *He wanted to know where the cinema is.*

Creíamos que era un vino chileno. — *We thought it was a Chilean wine.*

▼ Activity 2 — *The imperfect tense*

Put the verbs in brackets into the correct form of the imperfect tense:

a No le (importar) el precio.
b Nosotros (necesitar) el cheque ayer.
c Yo (saber) lo que (deber) hacer.
d Tú ¿adónde (creer) que ellas (caminar)?
e Él (aprender) mucho cada vez que le (enseñar) ese profesor.
f Ellos (salir) de la oficina a las cinco.

▼ The future tense

The future tense describes actions or events which will happen or are going to happen, e.g. *I shall speak, I will speak.*

▼ Forming the future tense

Future stem (which in the case of regular verbs is the infinitive, but which in all cases ends in **–r**) + future endings. The stress is always on the ending:

hablaré	comeré	viviré
hablarás	comerás	vivirás
hablará	comerá	vivirá
hablaremos	comeremos	viviremos
hablaréis	comeréis	viviréis
hablarán	comerán	vivirán

▼ Using the future tense

To refer to a very definite future event:

Estoy seguro que el avión **llegará** a tiempo. — *I am sure the plane will arrive on time.*

Les **veremos** mañana. — *We will see them tomorrow.*

A less certain or more immediate future is conveyed instead by the present tense:

Nos **encontramos** en el bar, entonces.   *We'll meet at the bar, then.*

- For legal or moral obligations:

Vd. **trabajará** de 8 a 1 y de 3 a 6.   *You will work from 8 to 1 and from 3 to 6.*

- To express possibility, supposition or surprise:

¿**Estará** lista ya?   *Do you think she is ready yet?*
¿Qué **querrá** decir esto?   *What on earth does this mean?*

The present tense is used in Spanish instead in the following cases:

When *shall/will/shan't/won't* express a desire or polite request, they are translated by the present tense of **querer** + infinitive:

¿**Quieres** esperar un momento, por favor?   *Will you wait a moment, please?*

shall in suggestions is translated by the present:

¿**Comemos** ahora?   *Shall we eat now?*

I am going to, etc. is frequently translated by the present tense of **ir a** + infinitive in Spanish:

Vamos a cenar.   *We are going to have supper.*

Also note the past form:

Iban a escuchar la radio.   *They were going to listen to the radio.*

▼ Activity 3 *The future tense*

Put the verbs in brackets into the correct form of the future tense:

a Los obreros (empezar) la tarea el jueves.
b Nosotros (atravesar) las montañas mañana.
c La criada (subir) la escalera en seguida.
d Ellos lo (permitir) sin duda.
e ¿Cuándo me (devolver) la calculadora, José?
f ¡Ya (ver) la diferencia, vosotros!

▼ The conditional tense

This tense describes what would happen (if . . .) e.g. *I would speak.*

▼ *Forming the conditional*
Future stem + -**er**/-**ir** imperfect endings:

hablaría	comería	viviría
hablarías	comerías	vivirías
hablaría	comería	viviría
hablaríamos	comeríamos	viviríamos
hablaríais	comeríais	viviríais
hablarían	comerían	vivirían

▼ *Using the conditional*
Basically the same as in English:

Nos **gustaría** descansar.	*We would like to rest.*
El **pescaría** si estuviera de vacaciones en Escocia.	*He would fish if he were on holiday in Scotland.*
Ella dijo que no **necesitaría** ayuda.	*She said she would not need help.*

The Spanish conditional can also be used to convey possibility, supposition or surprise when referring to events in the past:

Serían las diez cuando empezó a nevar. *It must have been ten o'clock when it began to snow.*

The conditional tense is not used in Spanish in the following cases:

- When the English *would* conveys a habit in the past. Use the imperfect instead:

Cuando estaban de vacaciones **comían** fuera cada día.	*When they were on holiday they would eat out every day.*

- The expression *would you like (to)* is translated by the present tense of **querer** when no condition is inferred:

¿**Quieres** tomar una copa?	*Would you like a drink?*

- *Would* indicating willingness in the past is translated by the imperfect or preterite of **querer**:

No **quería** esperar.	*He would not wait. (He did not want to wait.)*

▼ Activity 4   *The conditional tense*

Put the verbs in brackets into the correct form of the conditional tense:

a ¿Qué (tomar) si tuvieras un dolor de cabeza, Teresa?
(Tomar) una aspirina.
b ¿Cuál (escoger) vosotros si tuviérais el dinero?
(Escoger) la casa grande con la piscina.
c ¿Adónde (ir) Pablo y Marta si estuvieran libres esta noche?
Creo que Pablo (ir) a una discoteca y que Marta (visitar) a su novio.

▼ The perfect tense

This tense describes actions which have happened and are now complete. It is a combination of the verb *to have* with the past participle (see page 106), e.g. *I have spoken.*

▼ *Forming the perfect*
The present tense of **haber** + past participle:

he hablado	he comido	he vivido
has hablado	has comido	has vivido
ha hablado	ha comido	ha vivido
hemos hablado	hemos comido	hemos vivido
habéis hablado	habéis comido	habéis vivido
han hablado	han comido	han vivido

▼ *Using the perfect*
Basically the same as in English:

Paco **ha telefoneado** a su amigo.   *Paco has phoned his friend.*

Haber may never be separated from the past participle in compound tenses:

¿Se **ha duchado** Vd. hoy?   *Have you had a shower today?*

Note: the English expression *to have just (done something)* is translated by the present tense of **acabar de** + infinitive:

Ella **acaba de salir.**   *She has just gone out.*

▼ Activity 5   *The perfect tense*

Put the verbs in brackets into the correct form of the perfect tense:

a ¿Quién (jugar) al rugby? Nosotros (jugar) al rugby.
b ¿(Salir) hoy, Conchita? No, no (salir) nadie.
c ¿(Subir) los invitados? Sí, ya (subir).
d ¿(Beber) la sopa vosotros? No, no la (beber) todavía.

▼ The preterite (simple past tense)

This is another simple tense. It describes actions and events which took place in the past, for example, *I spoke, I did not speak, did I speak?*

▼ *Forming the preterite*
Stem + preterite endings:

hablé	comí	viví
hablaste	comiste	viviste
habló	comió	vivió
hablamos	comimos	vivimos
hablasteis	comisteis	vivisteis
hablaron	comieron	vivieron

▼ *Using the preterite*
Similar to English:

Se **levantó**, se **lavó** y se **afeitó**.	He got up, washed and shaved.
La guerra civil española **empezó** en 1936.	The Spanish Civil War began in 1936.

The imperfect tense is used instead in Spanish in the following cases:

- where the English simple past is used to describe settings or repeated actions in the past:

Salían juntos todos los sábados.	They went out together every Saturday.
No **tenía** ese coche la última vez que le vimos.	He did not have that car the last time we saw him.

- in most cases where verbs of wanting, thinking, knowing, fearing, etc. are being used in the past:

sabía	*I knew (fact, how to)*
conocía	*I knew (person, etc.)*
podía	*I could*
quería	*I wanted*
no quería	*I didn't want*

Sometimes these verbs even have a different meaning in the preterite:

supe	*I found out*	pude	*I succeeded in*
conocí	*I met/got to know* (people, etc.)	quise	*I intended*
		no quise	*I refused*

The translation of the English simple past in conditions is covered on pages 95–6.

▼ Activity 6   *The preterite tense*

Put the verbs in brackets into the correct form of the preterite tense:

a Ayer (vender) mi Seat y (comprar) un Rover.
b Anoche el Sr. Rodriguez (decidir) ir a Córdoba.
c Los clientes (firmar) el contrato esta mañana.
d El capitán (encontrar) el aeropuerto sin problema.
e Nosotros (comprender) en seguida las instrucciones.
f ¿(Mirar) en todos los sitios? [vosotros *form*]
g Desafortunadamente (quemar) el postre. [tú *form*]
h ¿Lo (aprender) todo, José?
i Vosotros (correr) mejor que el otro equipo.

▼ The pluperfect tense

The pluperfect tense describes what had happened (e.g. before another past event took place). It is another compound tense.

English example:

I had spoken.

▼ Forming the pluperfect
Imperfect of **haber** + past participle:

había hablado	había comido	había vivido
habías hablado	habías comido	habías vivido
había hablado	había comido	había vivido
habíamos hablado	habíamos comido	habíamos vivido
habíais hablado	habíais comido	habíais vivido
habían hablado	habían comido	habían vivido

▼ Using the pluperfect
On the whole the same as in English:

Habían comprado medio kilo de naranjas.	*They had bought half a kilo of oranges.*
Nos dijo donde **había encontrado** la carta.	*He told us where he had found the letter.*

The imperfect is used instead in the following cases:

• when the English pluperfect describes an action begun in the past and continuing into another action:

Trabajaba desde hace dos años como periodista cuando la conociste.	*She had been working as a journalist for two years when you met her.*

(See translations of *for* and *since* on pages 125–7.)

• in the expression **acabar de** + infinitive to translate *to have just (done something)*:

Cuando le llamé, **acababa de hablar** con el jefe.	*When I called him, he had just spoken to the boss.*

▼ Activity 7   *The pluperfect tense*

Put the verbs in brackets into the correct form of the pluperfect tense:

a   Nosotros (escuchar) la radio antes de salir.
b   No sabía dónde (estar) los prisioneros.
c   ¿Preguntaste quién (vender) la moto?
d   Yo (terminar) mi libro antes de acostarme.
e   No me dijiste que ya (corregir) las faltas.

▼ The past anterior tense

This compound tense has the same meaning as the pluperfect. You should be able to recognise it although you are not likely to use it in your writing.

English example:

I had spoken.

▼ Forming the past anterior
Preterite of **haber** + past participle:

hube hablado	hube comido	hube vivido
hubiste hablado	hubiste comido	hubiste vivido
hubo hablado	hubo comido	hubo vivido
hubimos hablado	hubimos comido	hubimos vivido
hubisteis hablado	hubisteis comido	hubisteis vivido
hubieron hablado	hubieron comido	hubieron vivido

▼ Using the past anterior
It is occasionally used in time clauses in literary Spanish instead of the pluperfect where this tense is contrasted with the preterite:

Apenas se **hubieron sentado** cuando el ministro anunció su programa.

They had scarcely sat down when the minister announced his programme.

▼ The future perfect tense

This tense describes what will have happened by a certain point in the future.

English example:

I will/shall have spoken.

▼ Forming the future perfect
Future of **haber** + past participle:

habré hablado	habré comido	habré vivido
habrás hablado	habrás comido	habrás vivido
habrá hablado	habrá comido	habrá vivido
habremos hablado	habremos comido	habremos vivido
habréis hablado	habréis comido	habréis vivido
habrán hablado	habrán comido	habrán vivido

▼ Using the future perfect
As in English:

Habrá ido de vacaciones antes de oír la noticia.

He will have gone on holiday before hearing the news.

It also indicates conjecture, normally when referring to things in the recent past:

Ya **habrá terminado** su trabajo.

He must have finished his work by now.

▼ Activity 8 — *The future perfect tense*

Put the verbs in brackets into the correct form of the future perfect tense:

a Creo que ellos ya (comer).
b (Llegar) los músicos, ¿no?
c Tú (reparar) la máquina antes de mediodía.
d Ella (soñar) en ganar el premio gordo.
e (Aprender) mucho en ese curso, ¿no, chicos?

▼ The conditional perfect tense

The conditional perfect describes what would have happened.

English example:

I would have spoken.

▼ Forming the conditional perfect
Conditional of **haber** + past participle:

habría hablado	habría comido	habría vivido
habrías hablado	habrías comido	habrías vivido
habría hablado	habría comido	habría vivido
habríamos hablado	habríamos comido	habríamos vivido
habríais hablado	habríais comido	habríais vivido
habrían hablado	habrían comido	habrían vivido

▼ *Using the conditional perfect*
As in English:

Creía que ella lo **habría mandado** por avión.	*He thought she would have sent it by airmail.*
El equipo **habría ganado** si hubiera jugado mejor.	*The team would have won if they had played better.*

▼ Activity 9   *The conditional perfect tense*

Put the verbs in brackets into the correct form of the conditional perfect tense:

a   No (tener) tanto sueño si se hubieran acostado más temprano anoche.
b   Suponíamos que el director lo (entrevistar) ya.
c   Yo te (acompañar) si hubiera estado libre.
d   Nosotros le (reconocer) si no hubiera llevado barba.
e   Tu mamá esperaba que ya (dar) de comer al perro, María.

▼ The subjunctive

All the tenses above belong to the 'indicative' mood. The subjunctive is another 'mood', or set of tenses, which is much used in both written and spoken Spanish although it has almost disappeared from English, appearing only in a few, mostly old-fashioned phrases:

Should he be found guilty, . . . (present)
If I were you, . . . (past)

It is also conveyed in English by words such as *may, might, were to, should.*

The subjunctive exists in Spanish to cover possible or as yet unrealised situations, to express doubt, emotion, the desire to influence events or another person's actions, and in a number of other cases, all of which are covered in greater detail below.

▼ *Forming the subjunctive – simple tenses*

Present subjunctive
To form this tense, take the *I* form of the present indicative and remove the final **o**, or **oy** in the case of a few verbs. The **-ar** verbs then add the present indicative endings of the **-er** verbs, and the

-**er** and -**ir** verbs add the present indicative endings of the -**ar** verbs. The only exception is the *I* form, which has the same ending as the *he/she* form:

hable	coma	viva
hables	comas	vivas
hable	coma	viva
hablemos	comamos	vivamos
habléis	comáis	viváis
hablen	coman	vivan

Imperfect subjunctive
There are two forms of this tense, one with endings in -**ra**, the other with endings in -**se**. They are used almost interchangeably but the -**ra** form is more common and is sometimes used instead of the conditional indicative tense.

Take the *they* form of the preterite and remove -**ron**. Then add the imperfect subjunctive endings, either -**ra** or -**se**:

hablara	comiera	viviera
hablaras	comieras	vivieras
hablara	comiera	viviera
habláramos	comiéramos	viviéramos
hablarais	comierais	vivierais
hablaran	comieran	vivieran
hablase	comiese	viviese
hablases	comieses	vivieses
hablase	comiese	viviese
hablásemos	comiésemos	viviésemos
hablaseis	comieseis	vivieseis
hablasen	comiesen	viviesen

Note the written accent on the **nosotros** forms to mark the stress three syllables from the end.

▼ *Forming the subjunctive – compound tenses*

Perfect subjunctive
Present subjunctive of **haber** + past participle:

haya hablado	haya comido	haya vivido
hayas hablado	hayas comido	hayas vivido
haya hablado	haya comido	haya vivido

hayamos hablado	hayamos comido	hayamos vivido
hayáis hablado	hayáis comido	hayáis vivido
hayan hablado	hayan comido	hayan vivido

Pluperfect subjunctive
Imperfect subjunctive of **haber** (-**se** endings) + past participle:

hubiese hablado	hubiese comido	hubiese vivido
hubieses hablado	hubieses comido	hubieses vivido
hubiese hablado	hubiese comido	hubiese vivido
hubiésemos hablado	hubiésemos comido	hubiésemos vivido
hubieseis hablado	hubieseis comido	hubieseis vivido
hubiesen hablado	hubiesen comido	hubiesen vivido

Conditional perfect subjunctive
Imperfect subjunctive of **haber** (-**ra** endings) + past participle:

hubiera hablado	hubiera comido	hubiera vivido
hubieras hablado	hubieras comido	hubieras vivido
hubiera hablado	hubiera comido	hubiera vivido
hubiéramos hablado	hubiéramos comido	hubiéramos vivido
hubierais hablado	hubierais comido	hubierais vivido
hubieran hablado	hubieran comido	hubieran vivido

■ Sequence of tenses
On the whole the subjunctive tends to be used in subordinate clauses (the 'secondary' part of a sentence which comes after *that . . .*, *until . . .*, etc.). The tense of the subjunctive depends on the tense of the verb in the main clause.
The following is a guide:

main clause	subordinate clause
present	
imperative	present
future	
perfect	perfect
future perfect	
imperfect	imperfect
conditional	conditional
preterite	
pluperfect	pluperfect
conditional perfect	conditional perfect ➤

Examples:

Dígale que **venga**. (imperative + pres. subj.)
Tell him to come.
Dudo que **haya ocurrido**. (pres. indic. + perf. subj.)
I doubt that it has happened.
Era improbable que lo **hubiese vendido**. (imperf. indic. + pluperf. subj.)
It was unlikely that he had sold it.
Esperaremos hasta que **termine** el concierto. (future indic. + pres. subj.)
We will wait until the concert finishes.
Les **pedí** que **subieran** al autobús. (preterite indic. + imperf. subj.)
I asked them to get into the bus.

▼ *Main uses of the subjunctive*

In the situations listed below the subjunctive is required in the dependent clause if the subject is different from that in the main clause. The dependent clause always begins with **que**. If the subject is the same in both cases, you can use the infinitive instead:

Quiero que me **compres** unas cebollas. *I want you to buy me some onions.*
(*I* is the subject of *want*, the main verb, but *you* is the subject of *buy*.)

but:

Quiero **comprar** una maleta.   *I want to buy a suitcase.*
(*I* is the subject of *want* and of *buy*.)

• After verbs of influence such as those expressing commands, wishes, requests, permission, prohibition, advice, etc.:

El médico le aconsejó que se **acostara** temprano.	*The doctor advised him to go to bed early.*
Dígale que lo **entregue** mañana.	*Tell him to hand it in tomorrow.*
Queremos que **traduzcan** el artículo al alemán.	*We want them to translate the article into German.*
Nos pidió que le **ayudáramos**.	*He asked us to help him.*

The following verbs may take an infinitive even if there is a change of subject: **hacer, mandar, dejar, permitir, aconsejar, ordenar, prohibir, consentir, rogar**:

Me permitieron que **aparcara** el coche aquí.
Me permitieron **aparcar** el coche aquí.

They allowed me to park the car here.

- After expressions of emotion or reaction: hope, regret, surprise, joy, fear, worry, etc.:

Siento que su madre **haya muerto**.	*I am sorry your mother has died.*
Le sorprende que no **hayan podido** reparar el reloj.	*He is surprised that they have not been able to repair the watch.*
¡Ojalá **hiciera** sol!	*If only it were sunny!*
¡Que **tengas** suerte!	*I wish you luck!*

The verbs **esperar** (*to hope*) and **temer** (*to fear*) may take the indicative or subjunctive:

Espero que se **hayan divertido**/se **divirtieron**.	*I hope they enjoyed themselves.*

- After impersonal constructions unless they express certainty:

No es verdad que **haya habido** una revolución.	*It is not true there has been a revolution.*
Era improbable que lo **hubiese dicho**.	*It was unlikely he said it.*

but:

Es cierto que les **ha tocado** la lotería.	*It is true they have won the lottery.*

▼ *Further uses of the subjunctive*

The following cases always have a subjunctive in the dependent clause, regardless of the subject, unless otherwise indicated.

- After doubts, uncertainty and verbs of saying, thinking or remembering used negatively, or in questions when indicating doubt:

Dudo que **sepa** esquiar.	*I doubt whether he knows how to ski.*
No dijo que lo **hubiese oído**.	*He didn't say he had heard it.*
¿Crees que lo **haya echado** al correo? (*doubt*)	*Do you think she has posted it?*
¿Crees que lo **ha echado** al correo? (*neutral question*)	

Statements where the main verb is positive and the verb in the dependent clause is negative are not affected:

Dijo que su padre no le **había escrito**.	*He said his father had not written to him.*

Similarly, clauses dependent on verbs of doubting or denying used negatively:

No negaron que **estaban** enfadados.   *They did not deny they were annoyed.*

Tal vez and **quizá** (*perhaps*) may take either the indicative or subjunctive:

Tal vez **sabes** (*or* **sepas**) su nombre.   *Perhaps you know his name.*

• After subjects like *nobody, not anybody, nothing, not anything,* etc.; or *somebody, anybody, something, anything,* etc.:

No dijo nada que **fuera** verdad.   *He didn't say anything that was true.*
Necesito alguien que **sepa** cocinar.   *I need someone who can cook. (i.e. anyone will do so long as they can cook.)*

Busca algo que **quite** esta mancha.   *He is looking for something (anything) to remove this stain.*

Los que **quieran** ir al teatro deben presentarse aquí a las ocho.   *Anyone wanting to go to the theatre must be here at eight.*

but:

Aquí hay alguien que **sabe** cocinar.   *Here is someone (definite) who can cook.*

Tiene algo que **puede** quitar la mancha.   *He has something (definite) that can remove the stain.*

Los que **quieren** ir al teatro deben presentarse aquí a las ocho.   *Those who want to go (i.e. have decided to go) to the theatre must be here at eight.*

• After certain conjunctions, or joining words, the most common of which are listed below:

*para que	in order that, so that	*a condición de que, con tal que, siempre que	providing, on condition that
*a fin de que, de modo que, de forma que, de manera que		a menos que, a no ser que	unless
como si, cual si	as if	*antes (de) que	before
*sin que	without	el que, que	the fact that
*en (el) caso que	in case	que	as far as
*de miedo que	for fear that	mientras (que)	as long as
no porque	not because		

Iremos al centro para que Vds. **puedan** hacer sus compras.	*We'll go into the centre so that you can do your shopping.*
A menos que **haga** buen tiempo, no vale la pena sacar la foto.	*Unless the weather is fine, it is not worth taking the photo.*
Hágalo antes de que **salgamos**.	*Do it before we go out.*
Que yo **sepa**, todavía no ha recibido el paquete.	*As far as I know, he still has not received the parcel.*

* If the subject of both verbs is the same, these conjunctions may
   be replaced by the following prepositions + infinitive:

para	sin	de miedo de	antes de
a fin de	en (el) caso de	a condición de	

Lo trajo para mostrárselo a ellos.	*He brought it to show them.*

▼ Indicative or subjunctive?

Clauses introduced by the following expressions take an
indicative when the statement is based on fact or experience,
and the subjunctive when dealing with future events and
hypothetical situations:

The conjunctions

cuando	*when*	hasta que	*until*
para cuando	*by the time that*	siempre que	*whenever*
después (de) que	*after*	mientras	*while*
en cuanto	*as soon as*	a medida que	*as (time)*
tan pronto como		aunque	*although*
desde que	*since (time)*	ya que	*since, seeing that*
cada vez que	*each time that*	a pesar (de) que	*despite*

Cuando **va** a España, siempre viaja en avión.	*When she goes to Spain, she always travels by plane.*

but:

Cuando **vayas** a España, no dejes de ir a Granada.	*When you go to Spain, make sure you go to Granada.*

Note that, if the subject of both verbs is the same, **después (de) que** and **a pesar (de) que** can be replaced by **después de** and **a pesar de** + infinitive:

Nos acostaremos **después de escuchar** las noticias.	*We will go to bed after listening to the news.*
A pesar de tener prisa, no tomó un taxi.	*Despite being in a hurry, she did not take a taxi.*

- **Por** + adjective/adverb + **que** (*however* + adjective/adverb):

Por lejos que **viva**, siempre llega a tiempo.	*However far away he may live, he always arrives on time.*

As this type of construction normally allows for an unlimited degree or quantity of the detail in question, the subjunctive is effectively used in most cases.

- Conjunctions ending in -**quiera** (-*ever*):

comoquiera que	*however, in whatever way*
cualquiera (*plural* cualesquiera) que	*whatever, whichever*
cuando quiera que	*whenever*
dondequiera que	*wherever*
quienquiera (*plural* quienesquiera)	*whoever*

Dondequiera que **va**, lo acompaña su perro.	*Wherever he goes, his dog accompanies him.* (It is known exactly where he goes.)

but:

Dondequiera que **vaya**, . . .	*Wherever he goes (i.e. wherever he may choose to go),* . . .

- The following type of construction always takes the subjunctive:

sea $\left\{ \begin{array}{l} \text{lo que} \\ \text{como} \end{array} \right\}$ sea	*whatever it may be, be it as it may*
pase lo que pase	*come what may*
diga lo que diga	*whatever he may say*
diga lo que quiera ⎫ beba cuanto beba ⎭	*however much he may drink*

▼ Activity 10   *Indicative or subjunctive?*

Put the verbs in brackets into the correct tense, determining whether the indicative or subjunctive should be used:

a Quiero que Roberto le (preguntar) otra vez.
b Su marido será feliz dondequiera que le (mandar) su compañía.
c Era una lástima que Paco no (encontrar) su reloj.
d Mientras mi hermano (quedarse) en Madrid, visitó muchos museos.
e Dámelo cuando (pasar) por aquí, Teresa.
f Cuando (vivir) en el Medio Oriente se quejaba del calor.
g No creía que el Sr. Pérez (salir) mañana.
h Dudo que Marcos (aburrirse).
i El pintor no se descansará hasta que (terminar) su obra.
j Hubiera preferido que vosotros (jugar) el sábado.
k Aunque Gloria (hablar) corrientemente el castellano, no es española.
h (Gritar) lo que (gritar), no le oirán a causa del ruido en la calle.
i Dejó las fotos para que nosotros las (mirar).
j El tren llegó a tiempo a pesar de que (nevar) bastante durante la noche.

▼ Conditional sentences with *si*

Type I

Where the English sentence *does not* contain a conditional tense (*would*, *would have*), implying that the 'condition'

i has already happened   ii might happen

the indicative is used in the **si** clause:

Si no te **gusta** el plato, déjalo.	*If you don't like the dish, leave it.*
Si **encuentra** unos tomates baratos, los comprará.	*If he finds some cheap tomatoes, he will buy them.*
Si **hacía** sol, ella pasaba todo el día en la playa.	*If it was sunny, she would spend the whole day on the beach.*

Type II

Where the English sentence *does* contain a conditional tense, implying that the 'condition' is

i imaginary, but possible   ii unlikely to happen

the **si** clause goes into the subjunctive:

Si **fuera**[1] / **fuese** rico, **compraría**[2] una casa grande.   *If he were rich, he would buy a large house.*

[1] imperfect subjunctive   [2] conditional indicative

Si **hubiera sido**[1] / **hubiese sido** } rico, { **habría comprado**[2] / **hubiera comprado** / **hubiese comprado** } una casa grande.

If he had been rich, he would have bought a large house.

[1] Pluperfect subjunctive   [2] Conditional perfect indicative or pluperfect subjunctive

Note that when **si** translates *if* or *whether* in reported speech, the indicative is used throughout:

Le preguntaré si **estará** en Roma.   *I will ask him if he will be in Rome.*

Le pregunté si { **estaría** / **había estado** } en Roma.   *I asked him if he { would be / had been } in Rome.*

▼ Activity 11   *Choosing the correct tense*

Put the verbs in brackets into the correct tense:

a Si (olvidar) de ir al banco, avísame.
b Te lo hubiera dicho si tú (estar) aquí ayer.
c Si (pensar) que iba a llover, llevaba su impermeable.
d ¿Hubiérais venido si (sentirse) mejor?
e Si Vd. (enviar) la carta hoy, llegaría a Roma el lunes o martes.
f Hubiéramos comprado un coche más grande si (tener) más dinero.
g Si (recibir) una cuenta, la paga inmediatamente.
h Si la Srta. Rodriguez no le (llamar), es porque todavía no ha terminado la conferencia.
i Me preguntaron si nosotros (probar) la cocina regional cuando estuvimos en Galicia.

▼ Giving commands (the imperative form)

English example:

Go! Let's go!

▼ *Forming commands*
Positive:

tú   the same as the 3rd person singular present indicative
vosotros   take the infinitive and change the final **r** to **d**

For **Vd.**, **Vds.** and **nosotros** the present subjunctive (see page 88) is used:

—	—	—
habla	come	vive
hable	coma	viva
hablemos	comamos	vivamos
hablad	comed	vivid
hablen	coman	vivan

Object pronouns are joined to the end:

Dígale.	*Tell him.*
Cómpralos.	*Buy them.*
Mándemelo.	*Send it to me.*

The **nosotros** form drops the final **s** and adds an accent when the pronoun **nos** is added:

Sentémonos.   *Let's sit down.*

The **vosotros** form drops the final **d** when the pronoun **os** is added:

Sentaos.   *Sit down.*

except in the case of **irse**:

Idos.   *Go away.*

Vosotros forms of -**ir** verbs require an accent:

Dormíos.   *Go to sleep.*

Negative:

The same forms as for the present subjunctive are used throughout:

—	—	—
no hables	no comas	no vivas
no hable	no coma	no viva
no hablemos	no comamos	no vivamos
no habléis	no comáis	no viváis
no hablen	no coman	no vivan

Object pronouns come before the verb in the normal way:

No **lo** comas.	*Don't eat it.*
No **los** saquéis.	*Don't take them out.*

▼ *Using the command form*

Basically the same as in English, as in the examples above.
It also appears in certain set expressions:

Oiga   *Hey, excuse me,* called to waiters, etc. to attract their attention; or *Hello* said as an introductory remark by a telephone caller.

¿Diga/Dígame?   *Yes, can I help you?* (shop assistant, etc. to customer); or *Hello* said when answering a phone call.

Tenga   *Here you are* (when giving something).

Sírvase   *Please* (on generalised written instructions, forms, etc.)

Mande (Mexico)   *Sorry/excuse me, I didn't quite catch what you said.*

¡No me digas!   *You don't say!*

¡Vaya + noun!   *What a (noun)!*

¡Fíjese/fíjate!
¡Figúrese/figúrate!⎫ *Good heavens!*
¡Vaya!⎭

Note:
The **él, ella, ellos, ellas** forms are preceded by **que** except in set expressions:

¡Que pase!	*Let him come in!*

but:

¡Viva el rey!   *Long live the King!*

▼ *When the imperative is not used*
• The infinitive is used in generalised commands or instructions:

No **tocar**.   *(Please) Don't touch.*
Ver capítulo XX.   *See Chapter XX.*

• The infinitive preceded by **a** is sometimes used in conversation as a general exhortation instead of the **nosotros**, **vosotros** and **Vds**. forms:

Bueno, amigos, ¡a **trabajar**!   *Well, friends, let's get down to work!*
A ver lo que dicen.   *Let's see what they say.*
¡**A dormir**, niños!   *Off to sleep, children!*

• The present indicative is used to make a command milder:

¿Me **das** diez pesos?   *Could you give me ten pesos?*

Here are some alternative ways of asking someone politely to do something:

¿Me puede/pudiera
¿Me hace el favor de ⎫ + infinitive?
¿Hágame el favor de ⎬

• The following phrases are also used as commands:

¡Cuidado/ojo!	*Be careful!*	¡Adelante!	*Come in!*
¡Ánimo!	*Cheer up!*	¡Fuera!	*Get out!*
¡Silencio!	*Be quiet!*		

• **Vamos a** often translates *let's*:

Vamos a ver (*often just* **a ver**).   *Let's see.*
Vamos a comprar un helado.   *Let's buy an ice cream.*

Vamos on its own or **vámonos** translates *let's go*.

▼ Activity 12   *The imperative*

Put the verbs in brackets into the correct form of the imperative, placing the object pronouns underlined in the correct position:

a   Dardo, ¡(pasar) <u>me</u> el azúcar, por favor!
b   ¡(Subir) Vds. ahora!
c   ¡(Vender) <u>se</u> <u>lo</u>, señorita!
d   ¡No (llorar) tanto, Juana!
e   ¡(Despertarse), Felipe y Pedro!
f   ¡(Casarse – nosotros form) en octubre!
g   ¡No <u>lo</u> (meter) aquí, por favor, señor!
h   ¡(Creer) <u>me</u>, Miguel!
i   ¡No (pisar) aquí, por favor, señores!
j   ¡No <u>la</u> (cambiar – nosotros form) todavía!
k   ¡No (esquiar) allí, jóvenes! Es peligroso.
l   ¡No <u>lo</u> (permitir), Tomás!

▼ Continuous tenses of the indicative

There are three continuous tenses in Spanish: present, imperfect and future. They are all compound tenses, consisting of the appropriate tense of the verb **estar** and the 'present participle'. How to form the present participle is explained on page 103.

English

The combination of the verb *to be* with the present participle (the *-ing* form), e.g.:

I am speaking.
I was speaking. (i.e. the same as the ordinary imperfect in English)
I will be speaking, etc.

▼ *Forming continuous tenses*

The appropriate tense of **estar** + the present participle, e.g.:

estoy hablando (present)
estaba hablando (imperfect)
estaré hablando (future)

▼ Using continuous tenses

To emphasise that an action is going on at a precise moment in time, often contrasted with another action which interrupts it:

¿Qué **estás haciendo**? **Estoy buscando** un número en la guía telefónica.	*What are you doing? I am looking up a number in the telephone directory.*
Cuando entró **estábamos leyendo** el periódico.	*When he came in we were reading the newspaper.*

Even in the above situations this tense tends to be used less than in English.

ir and **venir** do not have continuous forms:

Va a nevar esta noche.	*It is going to snow tonight.*
Ahora **vienen**.	*They are coming now.*

Unlike English, the continuous tenses are *not* used to describe planned future events:

Sale para Nueva York el día veinte.	*He is leaving for New York on the twentieth.*
Llegarán a eso de las ocho.	*They will be arriving at around eight.*

nor in letters or on the phone in the following types of expression:

Le **escribimos** para decirle que todavía no hemos recibido su paquete.	*We are writing to tell you we still have not received your parcel.*
Le **habla** Juan Otero.	*(It's) Juan Otero speaking.*

▼ Activity 13   *The continuous tenses*

Put the verbs in brackets into the correct form of the continuous tenses:

a ¿Qué (pensar) ahora, Carlos?
Yo (pensar) que debo lavar el coche esta tarde.

b ¿Qué (dibujar) Vds. cuando entré?
Nosotros (dibujar) un gato.

c ¿Qué (hacer) vosotros mañana por la mañana mientras estamos en la oficina?
Mónica (jugar) al tenis con su amiga y yo (pintar) el comedor.

d ¿Qué (describir) Vd. hace unos minutos?
Yo (describir) el hotel donde estuve ayer.

▼ The infinitive

This is the *to do* form of the verb, which you need to know to look it up in dictionaries, etc. Spanish verbs are grouped into three 'conjugations', according to their ending in the infinitive: **-ar**, **-er** or **-ir**.

For information about the position of object pronouns with the infinitive see pages 38–9.

▼ *Using the infinitive*

Directly after certain verbs (see the list on pages 54–6):

Desea **descansar**.	He wants to rest.
El olvidó **fregar** los platos.	He forgot to wash up.

After a preposition (note that in English the present participle is used, except after *to*):

después de **bajar** del coche	after getting out of the car
al **cruzar** la calle	on crossing the road
Trataba de **abrir** la puerta.	He was trying to open the door.
una máquina de **escribir**	a typewriter

As a kind of noun (see page 104), often translated into English by the present participle:

Ver es **creer**.	Seeing is believing.
A ella la encanta **hacer** punto.	She loves knitting.
No **fumar**	No smoking

As a translation of the English past participle or 'passive infinitive' (*to be done*) in the following types of construction:

Los vi **escribir**.	I saw them being written.
Hizo **construir** la casa.	He had the house built.
Hemos oído **decir** que ...	We have heard it said that ...
Hace falta **pintar** el comedor.	The dining room needs to be painted.
Es de **temer** que ...	It is to be feared that ...

▼ The perfect infinitive

English example:

to have spoken

▼ *Forming the perfect infinitive*
haber + past participle:

haber hablado
haber comido
haber vivido

▼ *Using the perfect infinitive*
As in English, but also where the gerund (the *-ing* form of the verb used as a noun) is used to convey a completed action:

Puede **haber sido** ayer.	*It may have been yesterday.*
Debe **haber terminado**.	*He must have finished.*
¿No recuerdas **haber**lo **utilizado**?	*Don't you remember using it?*

▼ The present participle as a verb

Where the term 'present participle' is used in general terms in this book, it means this verbal form. The adjectival form is explained in the next section.

English example:

speaking, e.g.: *He is speaking*, or *Speaking French is easier than speaking Russian.*

▼ *Forming a present participle as a verb*

stem + **-ando** (-ar verbs)	hablar – hablando
stem + **-iendo** (-er, -ir verbs)	comer – comiendo
	vivir – viviendo

▼ *Using the present participle as a verb*

• After certain verbs:

estar to form the continuous tenses:

Está **subiendo** la escalera.	*He is going up the stairs.*

seguir and **continuar** when meaning *to continue*:

Sigue **estudiando** la guitarra.　　*She is still studying the guitar.*

Continuará **trabajando** en la finca　*He will continue to work on the*
hasta fines de marzo.　　　　　　*farm until the end of March.*

Seguir is used more frequently than **continuar**.

ir meaning *to happen gradually*:

Mientras vayan **subiendo** los precios ... *As/while the prices (gradually) rise...*

llevar, mainly in time constructions (see page 126):

Llevamos dos meses **viajando** por　*We have been travelling around*
América Latina.　　　　　　　*Latin America for two months.*

- When one action is contrasted with another, or adds further information, as in the following examples:

Allí están, **mirando** el monumento.　*There they are, looking at the*
　　　　　　　　　　　　monument.

Salió **corriendo**. (See also page134–5.)　*He ran out.*

▼ When the present participle is not used in Spanish

- When the English present participle describes a position or completed action, the past participle is used in Spanish:

Están **acostados**.　　　　　　*They are lying in bed.*

- A present participle used descriptively after a noun in English is normally translated by **que** + the present or imperfect tense, as appropriate:

La secretaria **que está escribiendo** a　*The secretary typing in the corner ...*
máquina en el rincón ...

Tuvimos la habitación **que daba** al　*We had the room overlooking the*
parque.　　　　　　　　　　*park.*

- The English -*ing* form used like a noun is frequently translated by an infinitive (see page 102):

después de **cruzar** la plaza　　*after crossing the square*

Le gusta **pescar**.　　　　　　*He likes fishing.*

or by a Spanish noun:

la equitación	*riding*	las compras	*the shopping*
la natación	*swimming*	la calefacción central	*central heating*

▼ The present participle as an adjective

English example:

Speaking (as an adjective before a noun – see examples below).

▼ *Forming a present participle as an adjective*

stem + **-ante** (**-ar** verbs) entrar – entrante
stem + **-iente** (**-er, -ir** verbs) correr – corriente
    vivir – viviente
or occasionally + **-ente**: sorprender– sorprendente

Alternatively, with the exception of the last group it may be formed by changing the **-do** of the verbal present participle to **-te**.

It agrees like any other adjective. (See pages 19–20.)

▼ *Using the present participle as an adjective*

When the present participle is used as an adjective it agrees in number (singular or plural) but not in gender:

agua **corriente**	*running water*
la semana **entrante**	*this coming week*
papel **secante**	*blotting paper*
los párrafos **siguientes**	*the following paragraphs*
platillos **volantes**	*flying saucers*

You should always look in a dictionary when translating this kind of phrase, as often the Spanish version is totally different:

writing paper	papel de escribir
the dining room	el comedor
a swimming costume	un traje de baño
a tiring day	un día fatigoso

▼ The past participle

English example:

spoken

▼ *Forming the past participle*

stem + -**ado** (-**ar** verbs)   hablado
stem + -**ido** (-**er**, -**ir** verbs)   comido, vivido

In all cases except when used in compound tenses it agrees like
any other adjective.

▼ *Using past participles*

In compound tenses (see pages 75, 83–7, 88–9), e.g.:

Lo ha **encontrado**.   *He has found it.*

In the passive (explained later in this chapter):

La chica fue **educada** en Inglaterra.   *The girl was educated in England.*

It also translates the English present participle when the relevant
action is complete:

Están **sentados**.   *They are sitting.*
(i.e. have sat down and have remained sitting)

as opposed to:

Están **sentándose**   *They are sitting down*
(i.e. changing from a standing to a sitting position – action)

Other common past participles like this are:

acostado   *lying in bed*   colgado   *hanging*
apoyado   *leaning*   dormido   *sleeping*
arrodillado *kneeling*

As an ordinary adjective:

la torre construida en 1810   *the tower built in 1810*

▼ Reflexive verbs

Reflexive verbs describe actions done to oneself. In other words, the subject of a reflexive verb is also its direct object.

English example:

I wash (myself).

▼ *Forming reflexive verbs*

Reflexive pronoun + verb. Reflexive verbs are always listed in dictionaries, etc. in the infinitive and with the 3rd person pronoun, like this:

lavarse	*to wash oneself*

Present tense:

yo me lavo	nosotros nos lavamos
tú te lavas	vosotros os laváis
él, ella, Vd. se lava	ellos, ellas, Vds. se lavan

The only irregularity is with the first and second persons plural of the positive imperative (see page 97). The position of the reflexive pronoun is explained on pages 37–8.

▼ *Using reflexive verbs*

Some verbs are used reflexively only when they express an action one does to oneself:

Te has cortado.	*You've cut yourself.*
Ella se despertará.	*She will wake up.*

but

Has cortado la tela.	*You've cut the cloth.* (non-reflexive)

The following example, however, shows that the reflexive meaning is not always stated in English:

Me levanto.	*I get up.*

Reflexive verbs can also be used with parts of the body or clothing (see also page 123):

Se ha lavado las manos.	*He has washed his hands.*

Some Spanish verbs are always reflexive in form but without any reflexive meaning:

arrepentirse	*to repent*	jactarse	*to boast*
atreverse	*to dare*	quejarse	*to complain*
fugarse	*to escape*		

• Reflexive verbs can express action done to 'each other':

Se ayudaron.	*They helped each other.*
Nos aguardaremos.	*We will wait for each other.*

Sometimes this usage can be ambiguous:

Se ayudaron could mean (a) *They helped themselves,*
or (b) *They helped each other.*

So, if necessary, extra words can be added to make the meaning clear:

Se ayudaron **a sí mismos**.	*They helped themselves.*
Se ayudaron **el uno al otro**.	*They helped each other.*
Se escribirán **mutuamente**.	*They will write to each other.*

Sometimes, *himself*, etc. is added just for emphasis:

El niño se acostó **a sí mismo**.	*The child put himself to bed.*

Here is a list of all these forms:

oneself, etc.		*each other, etc.*
a* mí mismo	*myself*	(el) uno a(l)* otro
a* ti mismo	*yourself*	(la) una a* la otro
	⎰ *himself*	mutuamente
a* sí mismo	⎨ *herself*	recíprocamente
	⎱ *yourself* (Vd.)	
a* nosotros mismos	*ourselves*	
a* vosotros mismos	*yourselves*	
a* sí mismos	⎰ *themselves,*	
	⎱ *yourselves* (Vds.)	

*personal **a** (see pages 58–9) is used unless the verb takes any other preposition, e.g.:

Nos despedimos **el uno del otro**.	*We said goodbye to each other.*
(despedirse **de**)	

- Reflexive verbs are often used in Spanish to avoid the passive (see page 113):

Se rompieron dos sillas.   *Two chairs were broken.* (lit: *Two chairs broke themselves.*)

Certain reflexive verbs are always translated into English by the passive:

llamar	*to call*	but:	llamarse	*to be called*
encontrar	} *to find*		encontrarse	} *to be found*
hallar			hallarse	*to be situated*

- The reflexive pronoun **se** may be used with the 3rd person singular of a non-reflexive verb where an impersonal expression or the impersonal pronoun *one* or *you* is used in English:

Se puede ir a Africa en barco o en avión.   *One/You can go to Africa by boat or plane./It's possible to go . . .*

Se puede aparcar aquí.   *You* (i.e. anyone) *can park here.*

But when the verb is reflexive anyway, **uno** must be used as a subject:

Cuando **uno** se casa joven, . . .   *When one gets married young, . . .*

Si **uno** se despierta temprano, . . .   *If one wakes up early, . . .*

This is a very common construction in Spanish and is not considered at all stilted like the English use of *one*.

- The reflexive pronoun is also used as a deferential form of the first person:

¿**Se** puede (pasar)?   *May I come in?*

The reflexive pronoun is sometimes used in impersonal commands:

Véase página 73.   *See page 73.*

Tradúzcase al francés: *Translate into French:*

Many Spanish verbs become reflexive when used without an object. In some cases the reflexive and non-reflexive forms are translated differently in English. For example:

acostar	to put to bed	acostarse	to go to bed
casar	to marry (off)	casarse	to get married
detener	to detain, stop	detenerse	to come to a halt, stop
encender	to light up	encenderse	to catch fire
enfadar	to annoy	enfadarse	to get annoyed
levantar	to raise	levantarse	to get up
sentar	to seat	sentarse	to sit down
sentir	to feel (an object)	sentirse	to feel (ill, etc.)
vestir	to dress (someone)	vestirse	to get dressed

Certain Spanish verbs change their meaning when made reflexive. For example:

beber	to drink	beberse	to drink up
comer	to eat	comerse	to eat up
dormir	to sleep	dormirse	to fall asleep
hacer	to do, make	hacerse	to become*
ir	to go	irse	to go away
llevar	to wear, carry	llevarse	to take away
poner	to put	ponerse	to put on, become*
parecer	to seem	parecerse	to resemble
tratar de	to try	tratarse de	to be a question of
volver	to return	volverse	to turn around, become*

*See pages 123–4.

Others may be used reflexively or non-reflexively without any change of meaning. For example:

bajar(se)	to get off (vehicle, etc.)	reír(se)	to laugh
parar(se)	to stop	sonreír(se)	to smile
subir(se)	to get on/in (vehicles, etc.)		

Note the following expressions:

cantar para sí	to sing to oneself	leer para sí	to read to oneself
hablar para sí	to talk to oneself	sonreír para sí	to smile to oneself

▼ Activity 14   *Reflexive verbs*

Put the reflexive verbs in brackets into the correct tense and form:

a ¿A qué hora (levantarse) cada día, Pedro?
b Nosotros (llamarse) Arturo y Ernesto.
c ¿Qué hicisteis después de (sentarse)?
d Yo no (perderse) mañana porque tengo mi mapa.
e Nicolás (romperse) el brazo la semana pasada.
f Ellos no (aburrirse) anoche.
g Vosotros siempre (quejarse) de la comida cuando estábamos de vacaciones.

Make the expressions in brackets agree with the subject of the sentence:

h Estábamos sonriendo para (sí) mientras hablaba.
i ¿Estabas leyendo para (sí) cuando sonó el teléfono?
j Podemos vestirnos (a sí mismo) ahora, ya que nos sentimos mucho mejor.

▼ The passive

In an ordinary 'active' sentence the subject of the verb performs the action and the direct object receives this action. In a passive sentence the roles are reversed so that the noun which receives the action is the grammatical subject. The passive is not often used in Spanish.

English example: *It is spoken*, etc.

▼ *Forming the passive*

The appropriate tense of **ser** + past participle (which agrees with the subject like an adjective):

La ventana **fue abierta** por María.   *The window was opened by Maria.*

▼ *Using the passive*

• As in English, but much less frequent:

La chimenea **será limpiada** por la criada.   *The chimney will be cleaned by the maid.*
El asesino **fue detenido** por la policía.   *The murderer was arrested by the police.*
Los ejercicios **habían sido corregidos** dos veces.   *The exercises had been corrected twice.*

- *By* is usually translated by **por**, as above, but **de** is used after a few verbs:

La reina es amada **de** sus súbditos.	*The queen is loved by her subjects.*
El general fue seguido **de** otros oficiales.	*The general was followed by other officers.*
La casa está rodeada **de** árboles.	*The house is surrounded by trees.*
Siempre ha sido temido **de** sus empleados.	*He has always been feared by his employees.*

- When the passive is used to describe dress, emotions and timing, **ir** is often used as an auxiliary:

Va vestida de luto.	*She is dressed in mourning.*
Mi reloj **va** atrasado/adelantado.	*My watch is slow/fast.*

It is also frequently used with **acompañado** and **incluido**:

Va acompañado de su esposa.	*He is accompanied by his wife.*
Los impuestos **van incluidos** en el precio.	*Taxes are included in the price.*

Verse (lit.: *to see oneself*, meaning *to find* or *consider oneself*) is generally used with **obligado**:

Se vio obligado a decírtelo.	*He felt obliged to tell you.*

■ Avoiding the passive in Spanish

This may be done in a number of ways:

- If the agent (whoever *does* the action) is known, the verb can be made active but the word order remains much the same:

El anillo fue encontrado por Conchita.	*The ring was found by Conchita.*

changes to:

El anillo **lo** encontró Conchita.	*Conchita found the ring.*

Notice that a direct object pronoun is also needed in this construction.

- The impersonal *they* can be used:

Fabrican el coche en los Estados Unidos.	*The car is made in the USA. (i.e. They make the car ...)* ➤

- The reflexive **se** can be used – the verb agrees with what is now the subject:

Aquí **se habla** español.
Spanish is spoken here. (i.e. speaks itself)

This form may only be used when referring to things – otherwise an expression like **se mató** could mean *he killed himself* or *he was killed*.

Se may be used with people in the following way:

Se vio a la chica en el mercado.
The girl was seen in the market.

Se la vio en el mercado.
She was seen in the market.

To understand this form, think of the **se** as *someone*, i.e. *Someone saw the girl*. The verb, therefore, is always in the 3rd person singular.

This last form of **se** may be replaced by **uno** or **alguien** (*one/someone*):

Alguien me dijo que lo necesitaba.
I was told that he needed it. (Someone told me . . .)

- In English you can construct a second form of passive sentence, where the **indirect** object becomes the subject:

He was given the picture by Raymond.

(Raymond is the 'agent', the picture receives the action directly, 'he' receives the action indirectly.) This construction is impossible in Spanish. Instead, you must use one of the alternatives:

Le dijeron que no funcionaba el ascensor.
He was told that the lift was not working. (They told him that . . .)

Se le preguntó si tenía algo que declarar.
She was asked if she had anything to declare.

- Impersonal constructions in the passive are usually translated in the following ways:

se cree que — *it is believed that*
se dice que — *it is said that*
se sabe que — *it is known that*
se teme que — *it is feared that*
es de creer que — *it is to be believed that*

▼ Activity 15 — *The passive*

Put the verbs in brackets into the correct form of the passive:

a Las próximas casas (construir) de madera.
b Los ministros (asesinar) en Granada el mes pasado.
c La frase (añadir) antes por el gerente cuando revisó el documento.
d Su pelo (cortar) mañana por Luisa.

Now rewrite these sentences avoiding the passive.

▼▼▼

COMMON STRUCTURES
based on verbs

▼Ser/Estar *to be*

There are two Spanish verbs meaning *to be*, so it is important to know which one to use when.

▼ *Use of* ser

1 Before nouns or pronouns in definitions (i.e. in the question *what, or who, is x?* and the accompanying answer):

¿Quién **es**? **Es** Nicolás. **Es** él.	*Who is it? It is Nicholas. It is he.*
¿Quién **es** Paco? **Es** un arquitecto.	*Who is Paco? He is an architect.*
¿Qué **es** esto? No **es** nada.	*What is it? It's nothing.*

2 Before adjectives or adjectival phrases when describing something permanent or usual (such as nationality, religion, profession, colour, age, materials, ownership, normal appearance, etc.) and in questions requesting such information:

El azúcar **es** dulce.	*Sugar is sweet.*
El médico **es** francés.	*The doctor is French.*
El hielo **es** frío.	*Ice is cold.*
Su barco **es** pequeño.	*His boat is small.*
Es de plata.	*It is made of silver.*
¿Cómo **es** la cama?	*How is the bed?*
Es muy cómoda.	*It is very comfortable.*

By comparing these examples with paragraph 2 page 116 of **estar**, you will see that many adjectives can be used with either verb depending on the circumstances. The basic distinction to remember is that for permanent characteristics use **ser**, and for temporary characteristics use **estar**.

3 Before past participles to form the passive:

El palacio **fue** construido en 1957.	*The palace was built in 1957.*
El colegio **fue** fundado por el Conde de Manzanares.	*The college was founded by the Count of Manzanares.*

4 In expressions of time:

Es verano.	*It is summertime.*
Era de noche.	*It was night time.*
Son las seis.	*It is six o'clock.*
Es el 21 de diciembre.	*It is 21st December.*

5 With numerals:

Dos y tres **son** cinco.	*Two and three are five.*
La temperatura **es** de 20 grados.	*The temperature is 20 degrees.*

6 In most impersonal expressions:

es cierto que	*it is certain that*
es que	*the thing is that*
es de creer que	*it is to be believed that*

- *Use of* **estar**

(The numbering of the paragraphs is the same as for **ser**.)

1 Never before nouns or pronouns in definitions.

2 Before adjectives or adjectival phrases describing something unusual, temporary or reversible (for example, health, emotions, etc.) and in questions requesting such information:

¿Cómo **está** la sopa?	*How is the soup?*
Mi café **está** muy dulce.	*My coffee is very sweet.*
La botella **está** llena.	*The bottle is full.*
Su marido **estaba** enfermo.	*Her husband was ill.*

3 Before past participles describing the result of an action:

La luz **estaba** apagada.	*The light was off.*
El bebé **está** dormido ya.	*The baby is now asleep.*

4 With time – only in the following expression:

¿**A** cuántos **estamos**?	*What is the date today?*
Estamos a 2 de julio.	*It's 2nd July.*

5 With numerals – only in the following expression:

¿**A** cuánto **están** las gambas?	*How much are the prawns?*
Están a 500 pesetas el kilo.	*They are 500 pesetas a kilo.*

6 To indicate location (i.e. in the question *where is x?* and the relevant answer):

¿Dónde **está** el cine?	*Where is the cinema?*
Está allí a la derecha.	*It is over there on the right.*
¿**Está** el obispo?	*Is the bishop in?*

▼ Ser *and* estar *in certain set expressions*
Ser:

¿Qué **ha sido** de ellos?	*What has become of them?*
¿Cómo **fue** eso?	*How did that happen?*
Sea como **sea**.	*Be it as it may. (and similar phrases)*
Es igual. **Es** lo mismo.	*It's all the same.*
llegar a **ser**	*to turn out, happen, become*

When meaning to *exist:*

Pienso, por eso **soy**.	*I think, therefore I am.*
Dios **es**.	*God exists.*

Before **para** with the idea of purpose:

Las flores **son** para Vd.	*The flowers are for you.*
Es para beber ahora.	*It is to be drunk now.*

Estar:

estar de vacaciones	*to be on holiday*	estar de acuerdo	*to agree*
estar de viaje	*to be travelling*	estar de vuelta	*to be back*
estar de pie	*to be standing*	estar de luto	*to be in mourning*
estar de rodillas	*to be kneeling*	está bien	*it's all right*
estar de moda	*to be in fashion*	¿estamos?	*OK? agreed?*

estar para   *to be about to do something; to be in a mood for:*

Está para salir.	*She's just about to leave.*
No **estamos para** bromas.	*We're in no mood for jokes.*

estar a punto de   *to be just about to do something:*

Están a punto de pagar.	*They are just about to pay.*

estar por   *to have not done something yet; to be in favour of:*

Estoy por terminarlo.	*I have not finished it yet.*
Estás por vender el coche.	*You are in favour of selling the car.*

Before the present participle to form the continuous tenses:

Está cantando.　　　　　　　　　　*He is singing.*

A few adjectives have different meanings when used with **ser** and **estar**:

	ser	estar
listo	*clever*	*ready*
aburrido	*boring*	*bored*
pesado	*heavy*	*difficult* (person)
malo	*bad*	*ill*
bueno	*good* (by nature)	*well, healthy* (also **bien**)
vivo	*lively, quickwitted*	*alive*
cansado	*tiresome*	*tired*
divertido	*amusing*	*amused*
nuevo	*newly made*	*new, unused*
rico	*rich (wealthy)*	*rich (tasty)*

Some common expressions involving the English verb *to be* are translated by other verbs in Spanish. See the following:

hay (pages 119, 129)　　　　**tener** (pages 129, 143)
hacer (page 128)　　　　　　age (page 143)

Hallarse and **encontrarse** may be used instead of **estar** to indicate location:

La plaza de toros **se halla/se**　　*The bullring is at the end of this*
encuentra al final de esta avenida.　*avenue.*

▼ Other common verb structures

▼ *Hay*　there is, there are *(no plural form)*
This is a special form of the 3rd person singular present of **haber**. In all other tenses the normal 3rd person singular form of **haber** is used:

Hay un buzón allí.　　　　　　*There is a letter box over there.*
Había dos peras sobre la mesa.　*There were two pears on the table.*
Puede **haber** una pluma en el　*There may be a pen in the desk.*
escritorio.

Hay is never used before a definite article:

Existe el problema de su perro.   *There is the problem of his dog.*

Hay is also used in certain weather idioms (see page 129) and in a number of other common expressions:

hay que   *to have to (see page 121)*
¿Qué hay?   *How are things? What's up?*
¿Qué hay de nuevo?   *What's new?*
No hay de qué.   *Not at all, don't mention it.*

▼ Activity 1   *Ser or estar?*

Complete the following passage inserting the correct form of ser or estar:

… invierno. … el tres de enero. … de noche cuando Pablo regresó a su casa, que … en las afueras de la cuidad. Su casa … bastante grande y … rodeada de un jardín. … muy cansado y no … muy contento. … pensando en algunas cosas que habían ocurrido durante su día en la oficina. … para sacar las llaves de su casa cuando oyó un ruido raro. No sabía lo que … . El cielo … muy oscuro. Las luces de su casa … apagadas y no podía ver casi nada. Su mujer no … en la casa porque … de vacaciones con una amiga. Pablo … muy asustado. … seguro que había un ladrón en el jardín. Miró entorno suyo y vio lo que … . Llegó a … nada más que el perro enorme de su vecino.

▼ *Poder*   **to be able**

• English translations of the commoner tenses of **poder:**

present: *is able (to), can, may*
Puede hacerlo mañana.   *He can/may do it tomorrow.*
Pueden estar enfermos.   *They may be ill.*

imperfect: *was able, could*
No lo **podía** alcanzar.   *She could not reach it.*

future: *will be able*
¿**Podrás** estudiar el poema esta tarde?   *Will you be able to study the poem this evening?*

conditional: *would be able, could, might*
Vd. dijo que lo **podría** arreglar.   *You said you would be able to fix it.*

preterite: *was able, could*
No **pudimos** avisarle.   *We weren't able to let him know.*

perfect: *has been able, may/might have*
Ha podido conseguirlos.   *He has been able to get them.*
Podemos haberlo terminado.   *We may have finished it.*

- The English *can* or *could* is often not translated:

¿Me oyes?   *Can you hear me?*

- *May* is often translated by other expressions of possibility:

Es posible que ⎫
Puede que ⎬ apruebe el examen.   *He may pass the exam.*

Tal vez ⎰ se levantará ⎱ temprano.   *He may get up early.*
      ⎱ se levante   ⎰

or by requests for permission:
¿Me permite usar el teléfono?   *May I use the phone?*

or more informally:
¿Me deja fumar?   *May I smoke?*

and in some cases by the present subjunctive:
La policía teme que **esté** muerta.   *The police fear she may be dead.*

- While **poder** means *to be physically able*, **saber** translates *to know how to*:

No **puede** jugar al fútbol porque se   *He can't play football because he*
ha roto la pierna.   *has broken his leg.*
Gloria **sabe** nadar.   *Gloria can swim. (knows how to)*
¿**Sabes** tocar el piano?   *Can you play the piano?*

▼ *Deber* to have to *(moral obligation)*

- English translation of the commoner tenses of **deber**:

present: *must, should, ought*
Debe ayudarle.   *He must/should/ought to help him.*

imperfect: *had to, was supposed to*
Debía ayudarle.   *He had to help him.*

future: *will have to*
Deberá ayudarle.   *He will have to help him.*

conditional: *should, ought* (stronger than present)
Debería ayudarle.   *He really should help him.*

preterite: *had to, was obliged to*
Debió ayudarle.   He had to help him.

perfect: *has had to, must have*
Ha debido ayudarle.   He has had to help him.
Debe haberle ayudado.   He must have helped him.

- **Deber** also means *to owe*:
Me **debes** cien pesos.   You owe me 100 pesos.

- **Deber de** is used to translate *must*, etc. in the case of
  assumptions:
Salieron de Santiago a las once, así   They left Santiago at eleven, so they
que **deben de** haber llegado.   must have arrived.

In practice, **deber** on its own is often used with this meaning.

▼ *Tener que* + *infinitive* **to have to** *(neutral necessity)*
In impersonal constructions **hay que** is used instead.

Tuvimos que abrir la ventana porque   We had to open the window
hacía tanto calor.   because it was so hot.
Creo que **tuvieron que enviar** un   I think they had to send a telegram.
telegrama.
No sabían cuánto **había que pagar.**   They did not know how much they
                                               had to pay.
¿**Hay que entregar** el pasaporte?   Is it necessary to hand over one's
                                               passport? (Do I/we have to . . .?)

▼ **Activity 2**   *Can, must, have to . . .*

Complete, translating the phrases in brackets:

– ¿(*Can you*) ir al baile esta noche, Ana?
– (*Maybe*). ¿Cuándo (*does one have to*) llegar? No, tengo muchas cosas
que (*I must*) hacer. (*I have to*) terminar una carta a mi tía, pero también (*I
ought to*) ayudar a mi mamá en la cocina. Mis padres han invitado a unos
amigos a cenar. El problema es que (*I can't*) cocinar muy bien. ¿Me (*could you*)
ayudar?
– No estoy segura. (*I would have been able*) ayudaros esta mañana porque
estaba libre. Pero esta tarde (*I have had to*) prometer a mi mamá que haría
unas compras para ella y que arreglaría mi cuarto. ¿Te ha llamado, Isabel?
– No, (*she must have*) olvidado.

▼ *Haber de* to have to, it is arranged that

Habéis de ir a buscarles a mediodía.   *You have to go and fetch them at midday.*

¿Qué **he de hacer?**   *What have I to do?*

It can also mean the same as **deber de** or **tener que** in expressions such as:

Han de ser las tres.   *It must be three o'clock.*

▼ *Gustar* to like

- In the case of **gustar** and some other verbs, the English subject becomes the indirect object in Spanish, and the English object becomes the subject, with the verb agreeing with it. The word order is normally still basically the same as in English:

Me gusta la motocicleta.   *I like the motorbike. (i.e.: The motobike is pleasing to me.)*

¿**Te gustan** las manzanas?   *Do you like the apples?*

- **Gustar más** may be used instead of **preferir** *(to prefer):*

¿Cuál **te gusta más**, el vino blanco o el vino tinto?   *Which do you prefer, white wine or red?*

Me gusta más la cerveza.   *I prefer beer.*

- There are other common Spanish verbs which use this construction:

encantar *to like very much, love, be delighted with*

Les encanta dibujar.   *They love drawing.*

A ella **le encantan** esas faldas.   *She loves those skirts.*

faltar – when meaning *to be lacking, be short of, need*

¿Cuánto dinero **os falta?**   *How much money are you short of?*

Me faltan mil pesetas.   *I need a thousand pesetas.*

hacer falta *to need* (for a purpose)

Nos hace falta asegurar el equipaje.   *We need to insure the luggage.*

Te hacen falta unas zanahorias para el guisado.   *You need some carrots for the stew.*

quedar *to be left, remain*

Nos quedan cuatro días aquí.   *We have got four more days here.*

Le quedan mil dólares.   *He has got a thousand dollars left.*

doler   *to hurt, ache*

Me duele el brazo izquierdo.   *My left arm aches.*
Le duelen los dientes.   *His teeth ache.*

interesar   *to be interested in*

No **nos interesan** las noticias.   *We are not interested in the news.*

importar   *to mind*

No **les importa** la demora.   *They do not mind the delay.*

▼ Activity 3   *Special verbal constructions*

Put the verb in brackets into the correct form of the present tense and add the appropriate personal pronoun:

a   ¿A tus hermanos (encantar) volar?
      A ella (encantar) volar, pero a él no.
b   ¿Cuántos sellos (faltar) a Vds.?
      (Faltar) cuatro.
c   ¿Qué (hacer falta) hacer todavía en la oficina, Victoria?
      (Hacer falta) enviar un fax a una compañía en Buenos Aires.
d   ¿Cuánta gasolina (quedar) a nosotros?
      (Quedar) 15 litros.
e   ¿Dónde (doler), señorita?
      (Doler) aquí en la cabeza.
f   ¿Qué (interesar) más, jóvenes, los programas deportivos o los documentales?
      (Interesar) más los programas deportivos.

▼ To become + *adjective or noun;*
to get/go/grow/turn + *adjective*

There is no single translation for the verb *to become*, etc. but here is a guide to the most frequent ways of expressing this in Spanish:

- **+ noun**

through one's effort: **hacerse**

Se hará dentista.   *He will become a dentist.*
Se han hecho amigos.   *They have become friends.*

as a matter of course: **llegar a ser**

Llegó a ser general a los 50 años.   *He became a general at 50.*

indicating a change of nature: **convertirse en, transformarse en**

Torremolinos **se ha convertido en** un centro turístico muy importante.
Torremolinos has become a very important tourist resort.

expressions of time: **hacerse**

Se está haciendo tarde.
It is getting late.

expressions of age: **llegar a tener, tener, cumplir**

Cuando { **llegue a tener** 50 años . . . / **tenga** 50 años . . . / **cumpla** los 50 años }
When he turns 50 . . .

- **+ adjective**

deliberately: **hacerse**

Se hizo rica.
She became rich.

emotionally or physically – a quick, temporary change: **ponerse**

Se ponen nerviosos.
They get nervous.

Te has puesto rojo.
You've gone red.

Nos pusimos enfermos.
We fell ill.

as before, but more slowly or with lasting effect: **quedarse**

Se quedará ciego.
He will go blind.

Te estás quedando sordo.
You are going deaf.

But in many cases such expressions can be translated by a verb formed from the adjective. Sometimes these are formed by adding a suffix like **-ecerse** or **-ar(se)** to the stem of the adjective. In many other cases the prefix **en-**, **em-** or **a-** is also required, for example:

adjective	verb	
mejor	mejorarse	*to get better*
mojado	mojarse	*to get wet*
caliente	calentarse	*to get warm*
rico	enriquecerse	*to get rich*
enfadado	enfadarse	*to get annoyed*
loco	enloquecerse	*to go mad*
largo	alargarse	*to get longer*
peor	empeorar	*to get worse*

There are also other verbs that have this meaning when made reflexive, such as:

confundirse	*to get confused*	casarse	*to get married*
cansarse	*to get tired*	perderse	*to get lost*
aburrirse	*to get bored*	vestirse	*to get dressed*

▼ To make someone/something + *noun or adjective*

There are many ways of translating this into Spanish. Many involve the non-reflexive forms of the verbs used in the previous section:

Ese negocio no te **hará** rico.	That business will not make you rich.
El plato les **ha puesto** enfermo.	The dish has made them ill.
Vamos a **convertir** esta calle **en** una zona peatonal.	We are going to make this street a pedestrian precinct.
La multa le **enfadó** mucho.	The fine made him very angry.
El policía **te puso** muy nervioso, ¿no?	The policeman made you very nervous, didn't he?
Todo este trabajo me **cansaría** pronto.	All this work would soon make me tired.

▼ *Hacer* + *infinitive* to have/get something done; to make someone do something

Hacemos arreglar el coche.	We are having the car repaired.
Harán instalar una piscina.	They will have a swimming pool installed.
Eso le **hizo reír** a carcajadas.	That made him laugh his head off.
Les **hicimos callar** a los niños.	We got the children to keep quiet.

When someone else is being made to do something, **hacer** can be followed by **que** + subjunctive:

Haré que me **contesten** pronto.	I will get them to reply quickly.

If the action is being done to or for oneself, a reflexive verb can often be used:

El **se cortará** el pelo.	He will get his hair cut.
Ella **se ha hecho** un vestido.	She has had a dress made for herself.

Note also the following expressions:

hacer entrar	to show (someone) in
hacer esperar	to keep (someone) waiting

▼ *Translations of* for *and* since *in time constructions*

desde	since (preposition)
desde que	since (conjunction)
desde cuando	since when, how long (past)
desde hace	
hace (*time*) que	for (time leading up to a particular moment, either now or in the past)
llevar (*time*) + present participle	

With all these constructions, when an action begun in the past continues into the present, the present tense is used in Spanish:

El ascensor funciona **desde** ayer.	*The lift has been working since yesterday.*
Desde que está en Inglaterra, ha aprendido mucho inglés.	*Since he has been in England, he has learnt a lot of English.*
Están esperando la llamada **desde hace** una hora.	*They have been waiting for the phone call for an hour.*

The last type of expression may also be rendered in the following ways:

Hace una hora **que** esperan la llamada.
Llevan una hora esper**ando** la llamada.

and the question asking for this information may be put in one of three ways:

¿**Desde cuándo** están esperando la llamada?
¿**Cuánto tiempo hace que** están esperando la llamada? } *How long have they been waiting for the phone call?*
¿**Cuánto tiempo llevan** esper**ando** la llamada?

The constructions involving **desde hace/desde cuando** and **hace que** are the ones most commonly used.

- When the pluperfect (*had been*) is used in the English sentence, the imperfect is used in the main clause in Spanish, providing the action was incomplete at the time the second action took place. **Hace** changes to **hacía**:

Hacía dos horas **que** trabajaba cuando entré. } *He had been working for two hours when I went in.*
Trabajaba **desde hacía** dos horas cuando entré.

- When the first action is completed before or when the second action takes place, the same tenses are used as in English:

Habían estado en Alemania **desde hacía** cinco años cuando estalló la guerra. } *They had been in Germany for five years when war broke out. (implying that they then left)*
Hacía cinco años **que** habían estado en Alemania cuando estalló la guerra.

This often applies to sentences with a negative meaning:

Hace dos meses **que** no hemos ido al teatro.	*We have not been to the theatre for two months.*
Dijo que **hacía** tres días **que** no había podido dormir bien.	*He said he had not been able to sleep well for three days.*

- **Hace** also translates *ago* and precedes the unit of time:

Ocurrió **hace unas semanas**.	*It happened a few weeks ago.*
El bebé nació **hace seis meses**.	*The baby was born six months ago.*

- **Durante** translates *for* (duration of an action or state); alternatively, the preposition can be omitted:

La charla duró más de una hora.	*The talk went on for over an hour.*
Ha tenido la gripe **(durante)** tres días.	*She has had flu for three days.*
Estarán una semana en Asunción.	*They will be in Asunción for a week.*

Durante can also mean *during*:

durante la Semana Santa	*during Holy Week*

- **En** translates *for*, as above, but where an action has not taken place or is not expected to:

No les visitó nadie **en** cinco días.	*Nobody visited them for five days.*
No saldrá del hospital **en** una semana.	*He won't be leaving hospital for a week.*

- **Para** translates *by, for* when referring to a specific point in time:

La cita era **para** las diez.	*The appointment was for ten o'clock.*
Esta composición es **para** el lunes.	*This essay is for Monday.*
Ha vuelto **para** el cumpleaños de su hija.	*He has come back for his daughter's birthday.*

Para can also mean *for* after actions carried out for the purpose of spending time somewhere or using something for a period of time:

Se lo prestaré **para** una semana.	*I will lend it to him for a week.*
Lo necesitarías **para** quince días.	*You would need it for a fortnight.*
Han venido aquí **para** un mes.	*They have come here for a month.*

▼ Activity 4   *Time constructions*

**Complete the sentences below putting the verb into the right form.
Then supply a full answer incorporating the units of time given after
each sentence:**

a ¿Desde cuándo (vivir) en Inglaterra, Carmen?
  diez años
b ¿Cuánto tiempo hace que (marcharse)?
  cinco días
c ¿Desde cuándo creía que no (llover)?
  agosto
d ¿Cuánto tiempo (llevar) Vds. (trabajar) en ventas?
  ocho meses
e ¿Desde cuándo (ser) colonizadas las islas cuando ganaron su
  independencia?
  tres siglos
f ¿Hacía cuánto tiempo dijo que ella (estudiar) en la universidad?
  dos años y medio

▼ *Weather*

• Some verbs exist in their own right:

*helar	to freeze	lloviznar	to drizzle
*deshelar	to thaw	*tronar	to thunder
*llover	to rain	relampaguear	to flash (lightning)
*nevar	to snow	granizar	to hail

*These verbs belong to the stem change group (see pages 147–9).

No llueve ahora.	*It is not raining now.*
Nevaba ayer.	*It was snowing yesterday.*

Many expressions are made up of **hacer** or **hay** with a noun.
Hacer is normally used when there is no visible object:

¿Qué tiempo hace?	*What is the weather like?*	Hace frío.	*It is cold.*
Hace buen tiempo.	*It is fine.*	Hace fresco.	*It is chilly.*
Hace mal tiempo.	*The weather is bad.*	Hace viento.	*It is windy.*
Hace buen día.	*It is a fine day.*	Hace 20 grados.	*It is 20°.*
Hace mal día.	*It is a foul day.*	Hace 5 grados.	*It is –5°.*
Hace calor.	*It is hot.*	bajo cero.	

but also: Hace sol.   *It is sunny.*

Hay is normally used with a clearly visible object:

Hay luna.	*The moon is shining.*	Hay lodo.	*It is muddy.*
Hay neblina.	*It is misty.*	Hay tempestad.	*It is stormy.*
Hay niebla.	*It is foggy.*	Hay nubes.	*It is cloudy.*
Hay polvo.	*It is dusty.*		

In all the above expressions **mucho** translates *very* and **tanto** translates *so* or *as*. Both words agree with the noun as usual:

Hace **mucho** calor.	*It is very hot.*
Había **mucha** niebla anoche.	*It was very foggy last night.*
No hace **tanto** frío ahora.	*It is not so cold now.*
No hay **tantas** nubes como antes.	*It is not as cloudy as before.*

Estar is used in isolated idioms:

Está nublado. *It is cloudy.*   Está oscuro. *It is dark.*

▼ *Other expressions involving heat and cold*

• With people and animals: **tener calor/frío**

Tengo calor.	*I am hot.*
El perro tiene frío.	*The dog is cold.*
Tenía mucho frío.	*He was very cold.*
El gato tendrá tanto calor.	*The cat will be so hot.*

Mucho and **tanto** are discussed on page 47.

• With objects (always or usually hot/cold): **ser caliente/frío**
  (of variable temperature): **estar caliente/frío**

El sol **es** caliente.	*The sun is hot.*
El hielo **es** frío.	*Ice is cold.*
El café **está** muy caliente.	*The coffee is very hot.*
La cerveza **está** muy fría.	*The beer is very cold.*

▼ *Further idioms with* tener

Tener is used with certain other nouns where the English equivalent is *to be* + adjective, etc.:

tener cuidado	*to be careful*	tener miedo	*to be afraid*
tener la culpa	*to be guilty*	tener prisa	*to be in a hurry*
tener éxito	*to be successful*	tener razón (*fem.*)	*to be right*
tener gracia	*to be funny*	tener sueño	*to be sleepy*
tener hambre (*fem.*)	*to be hungry*	tener buena suerte	*to be lucky*
tener sed (*fem.*)	*to be thirsty*	tener mala suerte	*to be unlucky*

▼ *Some idiomatic uses of* **dar** *(to give)*

dar a	to look onto	dar la hora	to strike the hour
dar con	to bump into	Dan las seis.	It is striking six.
dar de comer	to feed	dar un paseo ⎫	
No me da la gana.	I don't feel like it.	dar una vuelta ⎭	to go for a stroll
dar un grito ⎫		¡qué más da!	too bad, never mind
dar voces ⎭	to shout, scream	darse cuenta de	to realise
Me da igual. ⎫	It's all the same	darse prisa	to hurry up
Lo mismo me da. ⎭	to me.		

▼ *Some other common verbs that are difficult to translate*

• *appear*

to come into view: **aparecer**

Apareció a la ventana.   He appeared at the window.

to seem: **parecer**

Pareces algo preocupado.   You appear a little worried.

• *ask*

to ask questions: **preguntar**

Le preguntó qué tenía en su maleta.   She asked him what he had in his suitcase.

The full expression for *to ask a question* is **hacer una pregunta**.

to ask for/after someone: **preguntar por**

Están preguntando por el gerente.   They are asking for the manager.

to ask for something (order): **pedir**

Pedí un bocadillo de jamón.   I asked for a ham sandwich.

to ask someone to do something: **pedir**

Le pidieron que se lo mostrara.   They asked him to show it to them.

to ask more formally (to request): **rogar**

Se ruega a los señores pasajeros no fumar.   Passengers are kindly asked not to smoke.

• *change*

to change money, exchange: **cambiar**

¿Se pueden cambiar dólares aquí?   Can youlls it possible to change dollars here?

to alter: **cambiar**
¿Puede Vd. cambiar la hora de la cita? *Can you change the time of the appointment?*

to change trains, clothes, mind, etc.: **cambiar de**
Tienes que cambiar de tren en Irún. *You must change trains at Irún.*
Se va a cambiar de camisa. *He is going to change his shirt.*

• *give*

to give (generally): **dar**
Les dimos las llaves. *We gave them the keys.*

to give as a present: **regalar**
Le regalará un collar para su cumpleaños. *He will give her a necklace for her birthday.*

to give in (i.e. *hand in*): **entregar**
Hay que entregar el trabajo hoy. *The work must be given in today.*

• *have*

before a past participle in compound tenses: **haber**
Ha comido. *He has eaten.*

possession, etc.: **tener**
Su hermana tiene una bicicleta. *His sister has a bicycle.*

when meaning to eat or drink: **tomar**
Vamos a tomar una copa de vino. *We are going to have a glass of wine.*

• *know*

to know people, animals, places, familiar objects: **conocer**
¿Conoces Buenos Aires? *Do you know Buenos Aires?*

to know facts/how to do something: **saber**
Sé cuánto cuesta. *I know how much it costs.*
La chica sabe cocinar. *The girl knows how to cook.*

• *leave*

to go out of: **salir** (**de** + noun)
Salen de la oficina. *They leave the office.*

to go away (people): **irse, marcharse**
Se fue sin decir nada. *He left without saying anything.*

to depart (trains, etc.): **salir**
El autobús sale de allí. *The bus leaves from over there.*

to leave somebody/something somewhere: **dejar**
Lo dejaré en la mesa. *I will leave it on the table.*

to leave unchanged, etc.: **dejar**
Lo dejamos así. *We'll leave it like that.*
Déjale en paz. *Leave him in peace.*

• *love*

to love people: **querer (a)**
La quiere a Elena. *He loves Elena.*

to love objects/doing something: **encantar, gustar mucho** or **muchísimo** (see page 123)
Le encanta la muñeca. *She loves the doll.*
Les encanta esquiar. *They love skiing.*
Nos gustaría mucho ir al teatro. *We would love to go to the theatre.*

• *play*

to play games: **jugar (a + definite article)**
Juegan al baloncesto. *They play basketball.*

to play music: **tocar**
Toca el violín. *He plays the violin.*

• *put*

to put (generally): **poner**
Póngalo aquí. *Put it here.*

to place with care/precision: **colocar**
Coloqué el vaso al lado del otro. *I put the glass next to the other one.*

to put inside: **meter**
Lo había metido en un cajón. *He had put it in a drawer.*

• *return*

to go back: **volver, regresar**
Han vuelto de Cozumel. *They have returned from Cozumel.*
Regresaremos pronto. *We will return soon.*

to give back: **devolver**
Devolvieron el paraguas hace poco. *They returned the umbrella a short while ago.*

- *spend*

to spend money: **gastar**
Hemos gastado mil pesos.   *We have spent a thousand pesos.*

to spend time: **pasar**
Van a pasar quince días en Grecia.   *They are going to spend a fortnight in Greece.*

- *take*

to take (most senses): **tomar**
Tome dos píldoras por día.   *Take two pills a day.*
Tome la primera bocacalle a la derecha.   *Take the first turning on the right.*

to take people/things somewhere: **llevar**
Te llevará a la estación.   *He will take you to the station.*

to take away: **llevarse**
Se ha llevado dos botellas.   *He has taken away two bottles.*

to take photographs: **sacar** (also **hacer**)
Sacaré una foto del puerto.   *I will take a photo of the harbour.*

to take out: **sacar**
Saca su pañuelo del bolsillo.   *He takes his handkerchief out of his pocket.*

- *think*

to believe: **creer**
Creen que se han perdido.   *They think they have got lost.*

to think (generally): **pensar**
Piensa mucho pero dice poco.   *He thinks a lot but says little.*

to think of (intend): **pensar**
Pensamos comprar otro coche.   *We are thinking of buying another car.*

to think of (have an opinion): **pensar de**
¿Qué piensas de la película?   *What do you think of the film?*

to think of (have in one's thoughts): **pensar en**
Está pensando en su novia.   *He is thinking of his girlfriend.*

▼ *Translating English verbs needing a preposition or adverb to complete their meaning*

- The prepositions or adverbs used fall into three categories:

1 Those which are added without changing the basic meaning of the verb:

open **up** = open   cover **over** = cover

2 Those which add to the original meaning of the verb:

go **back**, fly **back**, run **back**

3 Those which completely change the original meaning of the verb:

put **up with** (tolerate)   run **out of** (have no more of)

Verbs in the first group can usually be translated by simply ignoring the extra word, thus **abrir** = *to open* and *to open up*, and **cubrir** = *to cover* and *to cover over*.

The best way of dealing with the second group is to find a Spanish verb that conveys the meaning of the English preposition or adverb and then add a present participle, adverb or adverbial phrase to convey the meaning of the English verb.

For the third group you must use a dictionary unless you can think of another English verb which means the same and for which you know the Spanish equivalent, i.e. **aguantar** = *to put up with* and *to tolerate*.

- **Translation of the most common idioms of category 2**

English preposition or adverb	Usage	Spanish key element	Examples
across	motion	cruzar	*to jump across:* cruzar de un salto
			to fly across: cruzar volando (*birds*), cruzar en avión (*plane*)
away	motion	alejarse salir	*to swim away:* alejarse nadando
			to hurry away: salir de prisa
	continuity	seguir continuar	*to burn away:* seguir quemando
			to drink away: continuar bebiendo
	removal	quitar	*to blow away:* quitar soplando
back	motion (no object)	volver regresar	*to limp back:* volver cojeando
			to sail back: regresar en barco
	(+ object)	devolver	*to give (take/put/bring/hand) back*

down	motion	bajar	to *rush down:* bajar apresuradamente to *look down:* bajar la vista
in/into	motion insertion	entrar meter	to *ride in:* entrar cabalgando to *push in:* meter empujando
off	motion removal	alejarse quitar	to *walk off:* alejarse andando to *rub off:* quitar frotando
on	continuity	seguir continuar	to *sing on:* seguir cantando to *read on:* continuar leyendo
out	motion (no object)	salir	to *drive out:* salir en coche
	removal	sacar	to *take/bring out*
over	motion	cruzar	to *crawl over:* cruzar arrastrándose
through	motion	atravesar	to *cycle through:* atravesar en bicicleta
up	motion	subir	to *run up:* subir corriendo to *dash up:* subir de prisa
	completion	...(lo) todo	to *eat up:* comer(lo) todo to *sell up:* vender(lo) todo
		... completamente ... por completo	to *fill up:* llenar completamente to *finish up:* terminar por completo
	emphasis	various	to *dress up:* vestir(se) elegantemente to *cut up:* cortar en pedazos

Note:

When the verbs *to go* and often *to bring, take, step, come* and *walk* are used in this way, all that is required in Spanish is one verb. For example:

bajar = *to go (come/walk/step/take/bring) down*

Hacer and **dejar** can be combined with many verbs of motion with the following effect: **hacer** *to cause something or somebody to move in a given direction;* **dejar** *to let something or somebody move in a given direction.* E.g.:

hacer subir *to force up*   dejar entrar *to let/allow in*

▼▼▼ FURTHER INFORMATION

▼ Numbers

▼ *Cardinal numbers (one, two, three . . .)*

0 cero	19 diez y nueve,	90 noventa
1 uno, una	diecinueve	100 cien(to)
2 dos	20 veinte	101 ciento uno/a
3 tres	21 veintiuno/a	150 ciento cincuenta
4 cuatro	22 veintidós	200 doscientos/as
5 cinco	23 veintitrés	300 trescientos/as
6 seis	24 veinticuatro	400 cuatrocientos/as
7 siete	25 veinticinco	500 quinientos/as
8 ocho	26 veintiséis	600 seiscientos/as
9 nueve	27 veintisiete	700 setecientos/as
10 diez	28 veintiocho	800 ochocientos/as
11 once	29 veintinueve	900 novecientos/as
12 doce	30 treinta	1000 mil
13 trece	31 treinta y uno/a	1120 mil ciento veinte
14 catorce	32 treinta y dos	2000 dos mil
15 quince	40 cuarenta	10.000 diez mil
16 diez y seis,	50 cincuenta	100.000 cien mil
dieciséis	60 sesenta	1.000.000 un millón
17 diez y siete,	70 setenta	2.000.000 dos millones
diecisiete	80 ochenta	1.000.000.000.000 un billón
18 diez y ocho,		
dieciocho		

Note:

uno drops the **o** before masculine nouns, even in compound numerals: **un** día, veint**ún** libros.

1, 21, 31, etc. and 200, 300, 400, etc. have feminine forms: veint**iuna** casas, doscient**as** veinte pesetas.

ciento is used before numbers smaller than 100, **cien** is used on its own or before another larger number: **ciento** veinte, *but* **cien** pájaros, **cien** mil.

y (*and*) occurs only between tens and ones: *36* treinta **y** seis, *but 160* ciento sesenta, *204* doscientos cuatro. **Y** changes to **i** when 16–19 are written as one word and in the twenties.

millón and **billón** take **de** before a noun: un millón **de** naranjas, dos billones **de** dólares.

mil and **cien** are never preceded by an article: **mil** veces, **cien** árboles. **Mil** only occurs in the plural when meaning *thousands of*: **miles** de insectos, *but* seis **mil**.

The cardinals tend to precede the ordinals:

las **dos** primeras filas	*the first two rows*
los **tres** últimos vagones	*the last two carriages*

The digits of telephone numbers may be read out individually, but are frequently broken up into groups of two:

221.99.06   (el) dos – veintiuno – noventa y nueve – cero seis

▼ *Ordinal numbers (first, second, third . . .)*

first	primero (primer)*	*sixth*	sexto
second	segundo	*seventh*	séptimo
third	tercero (tercer)*	*eighth*	octavo
fourth	cuarto	*ninth*	noveno
fifth	quinto	*tenth*	décimo

These numerals agree like other adjectives and normally stand before the noun to which they refer, except in royal titles.

*****Primero** and **tercero** drop the **o** before a masculine singular noun:

el **tercer** mes	*the third month*
la **séptima** edición	*the seventh edition*
Carlos **cuarto**	*Charles IV (note the absence of the definite article in Spanish)*
Isabel **segunda**	*Elizabeth II*

Beyond **décimo** they are rarely used as they become extremely complex. The cardinal numbers are used instead, normally placed after the noun:

el siglo **veinte**	*the twentieth century*
Alfonso **trece**	*Alfonso XIII*

They are most commonly abbreviated by adding º or ª to the number, depending on the gender of the noun:

1ª clase   *1st class*   2º piso   *2nd floor*

▼ Collective numerals

We have a few collective numerals in English, e.g. *a couple* and *a dozen*. Spanish has many more.

All of these are followed by **de** + noun:

2	un par	100	un centenar, una centena
10	una decena	100s	cientos/centenares
12	una docena	1000	un millar
20	una veintena	1000s	miles/millares
30	una treintena*		

*30, 40, 50, 60, 70, 80 and 90 can be converted in this way.

▼ Fractions and percentages

Simple fractions

½ un medio*   ⅓ un tercio   ⅔ dos tercios   ¼ un cuarto

*half:

(noun) la mitad:	la mitad de la torta	*half the cake*
(adjective) medio:	media hora	*half an hour*
(adverb) medio (invariable):	Estaban medio dormidos.	*They were half asleep.*

Note also: un kilo y medio   *1½ kilos*   dos horas y media   *2½ hours*

Percentages

por ciento, por cien   *per cent*

Both are generally preceded by an article:

El treinta por ciento del país es árido.   *Thirty per cent of the country is arid.*
La población ha aumentado en **un 5%**.   *The population has increased by 5%.*

▼ Arithmetical signs

+	más, y	$4 + 6 = 10$	cuatro más/y seis son diez
−	menos	$10 - 7 = 3$	diez menos siete son tres
×	por	$5 \times 5 = 25$	cinco por cinco son veinticinco
÷	dividido por	$12 \div 6 = 2$	doce dividido por seis son dos

▼ Time

General expressions of **time**

¿Qué hora es? ¿Qué horas son?	*What is the time?*
Es la una.	*It is one o'clock.*
Son las dos.	*It is two o'clock.*

(from 2 o'clock onwards the expression is in the plural)

¿A qué hora?	*At what time?*
a la una	*at one*
a las tres	*at three*

Time past the hour:

la una y diez	*1.10*
las cinco y cuarto	*5.15*
las ocho y media	*8.30*

Time before the hour:

las diez menos veinte	*9.40*
las doce menos cuarto	*11.45*

In Latin America the following expression is frequently used:

Faltan veinte minutos para las diez.	*It is 9.40. (i.e. Twenty minutes are lacking for ten o'clock.)*
Falta un cuarto para las doce.	*It is 11.45.*

When referring to a timetable, time may be expressed as follows, using the 24-hour clock:

a las siete cincuenta y tres	*at 7.53*
a las catorce cero ocho	*at 14.08*

Periods of the day

mediodía *midday*	medianoche *midnight*
(de) la madrugada	*(in) the early morning (before dawn)*
(de) la mañana	*(in) the morning (later, or in general)*
(de) la tarde	*(in) the afternoon and evening (before 7 or 8)*
(de) la noche	*(in) the night (7 or 8 to 12 or 2 a.m.)*
a las cinco de la madrugada	*at 5 a.m.*
Son las ocho de la mañana.	*It is 8 a.m.*
Son las siete de la tarde.	*It is 7 p.m.*
Son las once de la noche.	*It is 11 p.m.*

■ Expressions of time

por la mañana	*in the morning*
por la tarde	*in the afternoon or evening*
por la noche	*in the night*
mañana por la mañana	*tomorrow morning*
ayer por la tarde	*yesterday afternoon*
el lunes por la noche	*on Monday night*
por la mañana temprano	*early in the morning*

but:

anoche	*last night*
esta mañana/tarde/noche	*this morning/afternoon/tonight*
muy de madrugada	*very early in the morning*
de día/noche	*by day/night*
anteayer	*the day before yesterday*
hoy	*today*
pasado mañana	*the day after tomorrow*
a las cuatro en punto	*at exactly 4 o'clock*
a las seis y pico a un poco más de las seis	*just after six*
sobre/a eso de/hacia las diez	*at around ten*
de nueve a una desde las nueve hasta la una	*from nine to one*
un cuarto de hora	*a quarter of an hour*
tres cuartos de hora	*three quarters of an hour*
media hora	*half an hour*
dos veces por hora	*twice an hour*

Days of the week

For Spaniards and Latin Americans the week begins on Monday. The days are all masculine and are written without a capital letter except at the beginning of a sentence:

lunes	*Monday*	jueves	*Thursday*	sábado	*Saturday*
martes	*Tuesday*	viernes	*Friday*	domingo	*Sunday*
miércoles	*Wednesday*				

el lunes	*on Monday*
los martes	*on Tuesdays*
los sábados	*on Saturdays*

All the days are the same in the plural except for **sábado** and **domingo** which add an **-s**.

Useful expressions

Mañana es viernes.	*Tomorrow is Friday.*
el fin de semana	*the weekend*
quince días	*a fortnight*
de hoy en ocho días	*a week today*
de hoy en quince días	*a fortnight today*

Months

All months are masculine and are written without a capital letter:

enero	*January*	mayo	*May*	se(p)tiembre*	*September*
febrero	*February*	junio	*June*	octubre	*October*
marzo	*March*	julio	*July*	noviembre	*November*
abril	*April*	agosto	*August*	diciembre	*December*

*You can write either **septiembre** or **setiembre**.

Dates

el primero de junio	*the first of June*
el dos de diciembre	*the second of December*

Note:

Cardinal numbers are used for days of the month, unlike English, except for the first which can be translated by either the cardinal or the ordinal. *The first of June* can therefore be **el uno de junio** or **el primero de junio**.

Día (*day*) may also be included in the above expressions, hence:

el **día** dos de diciembre	*2nd December*
sábado, el tres de mayo	*Saturday, 3rd May*

Nineteen hundred must be translated as *a thousand nine hundred:* **mil novecientos**.

De is inserted before both the month and the year:

el treinta de abril **de** mil novecientos noventa y ocho	*30.4.1998*

El is usually omitted in letter headings.

¿Qué fecha es hoy? Es el ocho de mayo.	*What is the date today?*
¿A cuántos estamos? Estamos a ocho de mayo.	*It is 8th May.*
en 1995	*in 1995*
los años ochenta	*the eighties*
10 antes de Jesucristo (10 a. de J.C.)	*10 BC*
50 después de Jesucristo (50 d. de J.C.	*AD 50*
or A.C. = año de Cristo)	

Seasons

la primavera	*spring*	el otoño	*autumn*
el verano	*summer*	el invierno	*winter*
en (la) primavera	*in spring*		

Miscellaneous expressions

el lunes (mes, año) pasado	*last Monday (month, year)*
la semana pasada	*last week*
en diciembre pasado	*last December*
el último mes	*the last month* (of a series)
la última semana	*the last week* (of a series)
al día siguiente	*the next (following) day*
a la mañana siguiente	*the next (following) morning*
la semana próxima/entrante/que viene	*next (this coming) week*
el próximo lunes / el lunes que viene	*next Monday*
el próximo mes de mayo / el mayo que viene	*next May*
el mes (año) entrante/que viene	*next month (year)*
cada día, semana, etc. / todos los días, todas las semanas	*every day, week, etc.*
dos veces al/por día (mes, año)	*twice a day (month, year)*
dos veces a la/por semana	*twice a week*

▼ *Translations of* time
Time in general: **tiempo**

No tengo **tiempo** ahora.	*I haven't got any time now.*
Duró poco **tiempo**.	*It lasted a short time.*

Time of the clock: **hora**

¿Qué **hora** es?	*What is the time?*
Es **hora** de comer.	*It is time to eat.*

One or more occasions: **vez**

tres **veces**	three times	de **vez** en cuando	from time to time
a **veces**/algunas **veces**	sometimes	esta **vez**	this time

A short period of time: **un rato**

Sólo tuvimos que esperar **un rato**.   We only had to wait a short time.

A long time: **mucho tiempo**

hace **mucho tiempo**   a long time ago
No tardará **mucho tiempo**.   It won't be a long time.

Historical period: **época**

en aquella **época**   at that time
en nuestra **época**   in our time

Specific moment: **momento**

en este **momento**   at this time

▼ *Age*

¿Cuántos años tiene? ⎫
¿Qué edad tiene? ⎭   How old is he?
Tiene 18 (años).   He is 18.
Me lleva 7 años. ⎫
Es 7 años mayor que yo. ⎭   He is 7 years older than me.
a los 25 años   at the age of 25
Va a cumplir diez años en marzo.   He will be ten in March.

▼ Measurement and distance

¿Qué longitud tiene … ? or ¿Cuánto tiene/es de largo … ?   How long is … ?
altura   alto   high
espesor   espeso/grueso   thick
profundidad   profundo/hondo   deep
anchura   ancho   wide

Tiene 10 metros de largo/longitud.   It is 10 metres long.
alto/altura   high
espeso/espesor/grueso   thick
profundo/profundidad/hondo   deep
ancho/anchura   wide

(In each of the above cases the adjective is invariable.)

| ¿Qué distancia/Cuántos kilometros hay de aquí a Ayacucho? | *How far is it to Ayacucho from here?* |
| De aquí a Ayacucho hay 400 km. | *Ayacucho is 400 km away.* |

▼ Conjunctions not explained elsewhere
▼ *Y*

| Pedro y María | *Peter and Mary* |

Changes to **e** before words beginning with **i** or **hi** not immediately followed by a vowel:

| padre **e** hijo | *father and son* |
| alemanes **e** ingleses | *Germans and English* |

but:

| acero **y** hierro | *steel and iron* |

Note that where English uses *and* to express combination, Spanish uses **con**:

| pan **con** mantequilla | *bread and butter* |
| whisky **con** soda | *whisky and soda* |

Also, where English uses *and* to express purpose, Spanish uses **a**.

Se sentó **a** leer el periódico.	*He sat down and read the paper.*
Ven **a** verme esta tarde.	*Come and see me this afternoon.*
Trate **de** conducir con más cuidado.	*Try and drive more carefully.*

both . . . and **tanto . . . como**

| **Tanto** los peruanos **como** los bolivianos hablan español. | *Both Peruvians and Bolivians speak Spanish.* |

▼ *O*

| jueves **o** viernes | *Thursday or Friday* |

An accent is added for clarity between numerals: 2 **ó** 3   *2 or 3*

Changes to **u** before words beginning with **o** or **ho**:

| siete **u** ocho | *seven or eight* |
| mujeres **u** hombres | *women or men* |

either . . . or **o . . . o**

| **O** está estudiando en la biblioteca **o** ha salido a comer. | *Either he is studying in the library or he has gone out to eat.* |

▼ *Que*

Que translates *that* before phrases or clauses introduced by verbs of saying, etc., and cannot be omitted as it can in English:

Dijo **que** tenías razón.	*He said (that) you were right.*
¿Cuándo abren otra vez? Me imagino **que** a las tres.	*When do they open again? At three, I imagine.*

Similarly, it may not be omitted when introducing a relative clause (see also Relative Pronouns on page 42–4):

Las peras **que** compraron son deliciosas.	*The pears (which) they bought are delicious.*

▼ *Porque*

Porque (*because*) should not be confused with **por qué** (*why*).

Como (*as*) should be used instead of **porque** at the beginning of a sentence:

Tomás está en casa **porque** tiene fiebre.	*Thomas is at home because he has a temperature.*
Como hacía frío me puse un suéter.	*Because it was cold, I put a sweater on.*

A causa de translates *because of:*

La fábrica está cerrada **a causa de** la huelga.	*The factory is closed because of the strike.*

▼ Suffixes

Diminutive suffixes are used mainly to make something smaller or to show affection or occasionally distaste.

Augmentative suffixes are used mainly to make something larger, but often clumsier or uglier.

Pejorative suffixes are used to make something more unpleasant.

The diminutives are the most common group.

The most common suffixes in each category are included below. They are attached to the stem of the original word, i.e. after any final vowel has been removed. Sometimes further changes take place. Such words should therefore be recognised rather than invented by students of Spanish.

Diminutives (affectionate; implying *little*)

-ito/ita

un poco	*a little*	un poquito	*a very small amount*
viejo	*an old man*	viejecito	*a little old man*
casa	*house*	casita	*cottage*
bajo	*short person*	bajito	*very short person*
un rato	*a short while*	un ratito	*a very short while*

-illo/illa

chico	*small boy*	chiquillo	*very small boy*
palo	*stick*	palillo	*small stick, toothpick*
campana	*bell*	campanilla	*small bell*

Augmentatives (implying *bigger*)

-ón/ona

hombre	*man*	hombretón	*hefty great man*
puerta	*door*	portón	*large door*

-azo/aza

gripe	*flu*	gripazo	*really bad bout of flu*
perro	*dog*	perrazo	*brute of a dog*

this suffix can also mean *a blow with*:

puño	*fist*	puñetazo	*punch*

-ote/ota

grande	*large*	grandote	*huge*
palabra	*word*	palabrota	*swearword*

Pejoratives (implying *worse*)

-ucho/ucha

cuarto	*room*	cuartucho	*poky little room*
blanco	*white*	blancucho	*off white*

-acho/acha

rico	*rich*	ricacho	*filthy rich*

-uzo/uza

gente	*people*	gentuza	*scum*

-uco/uca

ventana	*window*	ventanuca	*miserable little window*

-(z)uelo/a

autor	*author*	autorzuelo	*hack*
gordo	*fat*	gordezuelo	*small and chubby*

▼▼▼ IRREGULAR VERBS

▼ Stem change verbs

In Spanish there is a large group of verbs in which the last vowel in the stem changes whenever it carries the stress.

Group 1   -AR and -ER verbs

e changes to **ie**
o changes to **ue** } when the stress is on the stem
u changes to **ue**

Parts affected: present indicative and subjunctive, except 1st and 2nd person plural.

pensar *to think*		encontrar *to find*		jugar* *to play*	
present indicative	*present subjunctive*	*present indicative*	*present subjunctive*	*present indicative*	*present subjunctive*
pienso	piense	encuentro	encuentre	juego	juegue
piensas	pienses	encuentras	encuentres	juegas	juegues
piensa	piense	encuentra	encuentre	juega	juegue
pensamos	pensemos	encontramos	encontremos	jugamos	juguemos
pensáis	penséis	encontráis	encontréis	jugáis	juguéis
piensan	piensen	encuentran	encuentren	juegan	jueguen

*Jugar is the only verb where **u** changes to **ue**. **U** is inserted after the **g** in the present subjunctive to keep the **g** hard before the **e**.

Group 2   -IR verbs

e changes to **ie** } as in Group 1 above
o changes to **ue**

e changes to **i** } before ie, ió or stressed **a**
o changes to **u**

Parts affected: present participle; 3rd person singular and plural preterite; 1st and 2nd person plural present subjunctive; imperfect subjunctive throughout.

preferir *to prefer*			dormir *to sleep*		
present participle: prefiriendo			*present participle:* durmiendo		
present indicative	*present subjunctive*	*preterite*	*present indicative*	*present subjunctive*	*preterite*
prefiero	prefiera	preferí	duermo	duerma	dormí
prefieres	prefieras	preferiste	duermes	duermas	dormiste
prefiere	prefiera	prefirió	duerme	duerma	durmió
preferimos	prefiramos	preferimos	dormimos	durmamos	dormimos
preferís	prefiráis	preferisteis	dormís	durmáis	dormisteis
prefieren	prefieran	prefirieron	duermen	duerman	durmieron

imperfect subjunctive

prefiriera/prefiriese, etc.

imperfect subjunctive

durmiera/durmiese, etc.

Group 3 -IR verbs

e changes to **i**   when the stress is on the stem and before **ie**,
o changes to **u*** **ió** or stressed **a**

*There are no common verbs in this category

Parts affected: in all cases where the verbs in Group 2 are affected, namely: present participle; present indicative, except 1st and 2nd person plural; 3rd person singular and plural preterite; present, imperfect subjunctive throughout.

pedir   *to ask for*

present participle: pidiendo

present indicative	present subjunctive	preterite	imperfect subjunctive
pido	pida	pedí	pidiera/pidiese, etc.
pides	pidas	pediste	
pide	pida	pidió	
pedimos	pidamos	pedimos	
pedís	pidáis	pedisteis	
piden	pidan	pidieron	

Most stem change verbs have to be learnt and memorised. However, one clue as to whether a verb is in this category is if a stem change has occurred in a noun related to it which is also stressed on the stem:

almorzar*	*to have lunch*	almuerzo	*lunch*
comenzar*	*to begin*	comienzo	*beginning*
contar	*to tell a story*	cuento	*short story*
encontrar	*to find*	encuentro	*meeting*
gobernar	*to govern*	gobierno	*government*
helar	*to freeze*	hielo	*ice*
jugar*	*to play*	juego	*game*
morir	*to die*	muerte	*death*
nevar	*to snow*	nieve	*snow*
soñar	*to dream*	sueño	*dream, sleep*
volar	*to fly*	vuelo	*flight*

Other common stem change verbs
Compound and reflexive forms go like the verbs listed. Some of the more common of these have been included.

Group 1

acordar	*to agree*	aprobar	*to approve, pass (exam)*
acordarse	*to remember*	atender	*to attend to*
acostar	*to put to bed*	atravesar	*to cross*
acostarse	*to go to bed*	cerrar	*to shut*
almorzar*	*to have lunch*	colgar*	*to hang*
anhelar	*to long for*	comenzar*	*to begin*
apostar	*to bet*	contar	*to tell a story*
costar	*to cost*	oler	
defender	*to defend*	(o changes to **hue**)	*to smell*
deshelar	*to thaw*	perder	*to lose*
despertar(se)	*to wake up*	probar	*to try, prove*

devolver	*to give back*
empezar*	*to begin*
encender	*to light up*
entender	*to understand*
envolver	*to wrap up*
gobernar	*to govern*
extender	*to extend*
fregar	*to rub, scrub*
helar	*to freeze*
jugar*	*to play*
llover	*to rain*
morder	*to bite*
mostrar	*to show*
mover	*to move*
negar*	*to deny*
negarse*	*to refuse*
nevar	*to snow*
recordar	*to remember*
resolver	*to solve*
reventar	*to explode*
rogar*	*to request*
sentar	*to seat*
sentarse	*to sit down*
soler	*to be accustomed to*
sonar	*to sound, ring (bells)*
soñar	*to dream*
temblar	*to tremble, shake*
tentar	*to attempt*
torcer*	*to twist*
tropezar*	*to stumble*
verter	*to pour, spill*
volar	*to fly*
volver	*to return*

Group 2

advertir	*to warn*
consentir	*to agree*
divertir	*to amuse*
divertirse	*to enjoy oneself*
herir	*to wound*
hervir	*to boil*
mentir	*to lie*
morir*	*to die*
preferir	*to prefer*
referir(se)	*to refer*
sentir(se)	*to feel*

Group 3

conseguir	*to obtain*
corregir	*to correct*
despedir	*to dismiss*
despedirse	*to say goodbye*
elegir	*to choose, elect*
freír	*to fry*
gemir	*to groan*
impedir	*to prevent*
perseguir*	*to pursue, chase*
reír(se)*	*to laugh*
reñir	*to scold*
repetir	*to repeat*
seguir*	*to follow*
sonreír*	*to smile*
vestir(se)	*to dress*

*These verbs have other irregularities, explained below.

▼ *Spelling change verbs*

These are verbs with spelling changes that follow the rules set out on pages 1–4 and which in some cases also have the odd minor irregularity. The verbs are listed according to their endings.

- **-car**

c changes to **qu** before **e**

Parts affected: 1st person singular preterite; all of present subjunctive.

buscar *to look for*

preterite: bus**qu**é
present subjunctive: bus**qu**e, etc.

- **-zar**

z changes to **c** before **e**

Parts affected: 1st person singular preterite; all of present subjunctive.

cruzar   *to cross*

preterite:	crucé
present subjunctive:	cruce, etc.

- **-quir**

qu changes to **c** before **a** or **o**

Parts affected: 1st person singular present indicative; all of present subjunctive.

delinquir   *to commit an offence*

present indicative:	delinco
present subjunctive:	delinca, etc.

- **consonant + -cer, -cir**

c changes to **z** before **a** or **o**

Parts affected: 1st person singular present indicative; all of present subjunctive.

vencer   *to defeat*

present indicative:	venzo
present subjunctive:	venza, etc.

- **vowel + -cer, -cir** (for **-ducir** see below)

add **z** before **-co, -ca**

Parts affected: 1st person singular present indicative; all of present subjunctive.

conocer   *to know*

present indicative:	conozco
present subjunctive:	conozca, etc.

Some common exceptions:

hacer, decir, satisfacer

- **-ducir**

add **z** before **-co, -ca**

Parts affected: 1st person singular present indicative; all of present subjunctive. They also have an irregular preterite, and consequently imperfect subjunctive.

traducir   *to translate*

present indicative:	traduzco
present subjunctive:	traduzca, etc.
preterite:	traduje, tradujiste, tradujo, tradujimos, tradujisteis, tradujeron
imperfect subjunctive:	tradujera, tradujese, etc.

- **-gar**

g changes to **gu** before **e**

Parts affected: 1st person singular preterite; all of present subjunctive.

pagar   *to pay*

preterite:	pagué
present subjunctive:	pague, etc.

- **-guar**

gu changes to **gü** before **e**

Parts affected: 1st person singular preterite; all of present subjunctive.

averiguar   *to find out*

| *preterite:* | averi**gü**é |
| *present subjunctive:* | averi**gü**e, etc. |

- **-ger, -gir**

g changes to **j** before **a** or **o**

Parts affected: 1st person singular present indicative; all of present subjunctive.

proteger   *to protect*

| *present indicative:* | prote**j**o |
| *present subjunctive:* | prote**j**a, etc. |

- **-guir**

gu changes to **g** before **a** or **o**

Parts affected: 1st person singular present indicative; all of present subjunctive.

distinguir   *to distinguish*

| *present indicative:* | distin**g**o |
| *present subjunctive:* | distin**g**a, etc. |

- **-uir** (other than **-guir** and **-quir** above)

i changes to **y** when unaccented and between two or more vowels:

construir   *to build*

present participle:	constru**y**endo
past participle:	construido
present indicative:	constru**y**o, constru**y**es, constru**y**e, construimos, construís, constru**y**en
imperfect:	construía, etc.
future:	construiré, etc.
conditional:	construiría, etc.
preterite:	construí, construiste, constru**y**ó, construimos, construisteis, constru**y**eron
present subjunctive:	constru**y**a, etc.
imperfect subjunctive:	constru**y**era/constru**y**ese, etc.
imperative:	constru**y**e (tú), construid (vosotros)

- **-güir**

i changes to **y** as with the previous group.
gü changes to **gu** before **y**

argüir   *to argue*

present participle:	ar**gu**yendo
past participle:	argüido
present indicative:	ar**gu**yo, ar**gu**yes, ar**gu**ye, argüimos, argüís, ar**gu**yen
imperfect:	argüía, etc.
future:	argüiré, etc.
conditional	argüiría, etc.

preterite:	argüí, argüiste, ar**gu**yó, argüimos, argüisteis, ar**gu**yeron
present subjunctive:	ar**gu**ya, etc.
imperfect subjunctive:	ar**gu**yera/ar**gu**yese, etc.
imperative:	ar**gu**ye (tú), argüid (vosotros)

• -eer

i becomes accented whenever stressed
unaccented **i** changes to **y**

Parts affected: participles; imperfect; preterite; imperfect subjunctive.

creer   *to believe*

present participle:	cre**y**endo
past participle:	creído
imperfect:	creía, etc.
preterite:	creí, creíste, cre**y**ó, creímos, creísteis, cre**y**eron
imperfect subjunctive:	cre**y**era/cre**y**ese, etc.

Note: each **e** is pronounced separately: cre–er, cre–e, etc.

• -llir, -ñer, -ñir

unstressed **i** is dropped when it follows **ll** or **ñ**

Parts affected: present participle; 3rd person singular and plural preterite; all of imperfect subjunctive.

	bullir *to boil*	gruñir *to groan*
present participle:	bullendo	gruñendo
preterite:	bulló, bulleron	gruño, gruñeron
imperfect subjunctive:	bullera/bullese, etc.	gruñera/gruñese, etc.

• -iar, -uar (*but not* -cuar, -guar)

some of these verbs are stressed on the **i** or **u** when the stress is on the stem.

Parts affected: present indicative and subjunctive except 1st and 2nd persons plural.

enviar   *to send*

| *present indicative:* | envío, envías, envía, enviamos, enviáis, envían |
| *present subjunctive:* | envíe, envíes, envíe, enviemos, enviéis, envíen |

continuar   *to continue*

| *present indicative:* | continúo, continúas, continúa continuamos, continuáis, continúan |
| *present subjunctive:* | continúe, continúes, continúe continuemos, continuéis, continúen |

Other common verbs in this category:

criar	*to bring up, raise*	guiar	*to guide*
enfriar	*to cool down*	liar	*to tie*
espiar	*to spy on*	vaciar	*to empty*
esquiar	*to ski*	variar	*to vary*
fiar	*to trust*	(and compounds)	
actuar	*to act*	situar	*to situate*
efectuar	*to carry out*		

Common verbs **not** in this category:

anunciar	*to announce*	estudiar	*to study*
apreciar	*to appreciate*	financiar	*to finance*
cambiar	*to change*	limpiar	*to clean*
despreciar	*to despise*	negociar	*to negotiate*
divorciar	*to divorce*	odiar	*to hate*
envidiar	*to envy*	pronunciar	*to pronounce*

The **i** or **u** of the stem of the following verbs is accented to show that it carries the stress (see Accents on page 6):

aislar	*to isolate*	reunir	*to reunite*
prohibir	*to prohibit*	rehusar	*to refuse*

present indicative: aíslo, aíslas, aísla, aislamos, aisláis, aíslan
present subjunctive: aísle, aísles, aísle, aislemos, aisléis, aíslen
present indicative: reúno, reúnes, reúne, reunimos, reunís, reúnen
present subjunctive: reúna, reúnas, reúna, reunamos, reunáis, reúnan

▼ *Verbs with irregular past participles*

Some common verbs have irregular past participles but are otherwise regular:

abrir	*to open*	abierto
cubrir	*to cover*	cubierto
describir	*to describe*	descrito
escribir	*to write*	escrito
imprimir	*to print*	impreso
proveer	*to provide*	provisto
romper	*to break*	roto

A few stem change verbs have irregular past participles:

freír	*to fry*	frito* (otherwise like reír)
morir	*to die*	muerto
resolver	*to solve, resolve*	resuelto
volver	*to return*	vuelto

and compounds of both the above groups.

*This form is only used as an adjective:

patatas **fritas**	*fried potatoes (chips)*

but:

Ha **freído** unas patatas.	*She has fried some potatoes.*

▼ *Common irregular verbs*

The parts of the verbs given on the following pages are the minimum needed to form all the tenses. For all other parts see the chapter about verbs.

Verb forms which are irregular are printed in heavy type.

Verbs derived from these irregular verbs behave in the same way, so, for example, **proponer** (*to propose*) and **suponer** (*to suppose*) go like **poner**. In addition, **satisfacer** (*to satisfy*) goes like **hacer**. Verbs ending in **-dar** and **-ir** do not behave like **dar** and **ir** as they are not true compounds. **Bendecir** (*to bless*) and **maldecir** (*to curse*) have regular past participles, **bendecido** and **maldecido**, but otherwise go like **decir**.

Infinitive present participle past participle	present indicative	imperfect	future	conditional
andar *to walk*	ando	andaba	andaré	andaría
caber *to fit* cabiendo cabido	**quepo** cabes cabe cabemos cabéis caben	cabía	**cabré**	**cabría**
caer *to call* **cayendo** caído	**caigo** caes cae caemos caéis caen	caía	caeré	caería
dar *to give* dando dado	**doy** das da damos dais dan	daba	daré	daría
decir *to say* diciendo **dicho**	**digo** dices dice decimos decís dicen	decía	**diré**	**diría**
estar *to be* estando estado	**estoy** **estás** **está** estamos estáis **están**	estaba	estaré	estaría
haber *to have* habiendo habido	**he** **has** **ha** **hemos** habéis **han**	había	**habré**	**habría**
hacer *to do, make* haciendo **hecho**	**hago** haces hace hacemos hacéis hacen	hacía	**haré**	**haría**

preterite	present subjunctive	imperfect subjunctive	imperative
anduve	ande	anduviera/anduviese	ande
anduviste			
anduvo			
anduvimos			
anduvisteis			
anduvieron			
cupe	quepa	cupiera/cupiese	
cupiste	quepas		cabe
cupo	quepa		
cupimos	quepamos		
cupisteis	quepáis		cabed
cupieron	quepan		
caí	caiga	cayera/cayese	
caíste	caigas		cae
cayó	caiga		
caímos	caigamos		
caísteis	caigáis		caed
cayeron	caigan		
di	dé	diera/diese	
diste	des		da
dio	dé		
dimos	demos		
disteis	deis		dad
dieron	den		
dije	diga	dijera/dijese	
dijiste	digas		di
dijo	diga		
dijimos	digamos		
dijisteis	digáis		decid
dijeron	digan		
estuve	esté	estuviera/estuviese	
estuviste	estés		está
estuvo	esté		
estuvimos	estemos		
estuvisteis	estéis		estad
estuvieron	estén		
hube	haya	hubiera/hubiese	
hubiste	hayas		he
hubo	haya		
hubimos	hayamos		
hubisteis	hayáis		habed
hubieron	hayan		
hice	haga	hiciera/hiciese	
hiciste	hagas		haz
hizo	haga		
hicimos	hagamos		
hicisteis	hagáis		haced
hicieron	hagan		

infinitive present participle past participle	present indicative	imperfect	future	conditional
ir *to go* **yendo** ido	**voy** **vas** **va** **vamos** **vais** **van**	**iba** **ibas** **iba** **íbamos** **ibais** **iban**	iré	iría
oír *to hear* **oyendo** oído	**oigo** **oyes** **oye** oímos oís **oyen**	oía	oiré	oiría
poder *to be able* **pudiendo** podido	**puedo** **puedes** **puede** podemos podéis **pueden**	podía	**podré**	**podría**
poner *to put* poniendo **puesto**	**pongo** pones pone ponemos ponéis ponen	ponía	**pondré**	**pondría**
querer *to want* queriendo querido	**quiero** **quieres** **quiere** queremos queréis **quieren**	quería	**querré**	**querría**
reír *to laugh* **riendo** reído	**río** **ríes** **ríe** reímos reís **rien**	reía	reiré	reiría
saber *to know* sabiendo sabido	**sé** sabes sabe sabemos sabéis saben	sabía	**sabré**	**sabría**

preterite	present subjunctive	imperfect subjunctive	imperative
fue	vaya	fuera/fuese	
fuiste	vayas		ve
fue	vaya		
fuimos	vayamos		
fuisteis	vayáis		id
fueron	vayan		
oí	oiga	oyera/oyese	
oíste	oigas		oye
oyó	oiga		
oímos	oigamos		
oísteis	oigáis		oíd
oyeron	oigan		
pude	pueda	pudiera/pudiese	
pudiste	puedas		puede
pudo	pueda		
pudimos	podamos		
pudisteis	podáis		poded
pudieron	puedan		
puse	ponga	pusiera/pusiese	
pusiste	pongas		pon
puso	ponga		
pusimos	pongamos		
pusisteis	pongáis		poned
pusieron	pongan		
quise	quiera	quisiera/quisiese	
quisiste	quieras		quiere
quiso	quiera		
quisimos	queramos		
quisisteis	queráis		quered
quisieron	quieran		
reí	ría	riera/riese	
reíste	rías		ríe
rio	ría		
reímos	riamos		
reísteis	riáis		reíd
rieron	rían		
supe	sepa	supiera/supiese	
supiste	sepas		sabe
supo	sepa		
supimos	sepamos		
supisteis	sepáis		sabed
supieron	sepan		

infinitive present participle past participle	present indicative	imperfect	future	conditional
salir *to go out* saliendo salido	**salgo** sales sale salimos salís salen	salía	**saldré**	**saldría**
ser *to be* siendo sido	**soy** **eres** **es** **somos** **sois** **son**	**era** **eras** **era** **éramos** **erais** **eran**	seré	sería
tener *to have* teniendo tenido	**tengo** **tienes** **tiene** tenemos tenéis **tienen**	tenía	**tendré**	**tendría**
traer *to bring* **trayendo** traído	**traigo** traes trae traemos traéis traen	traía	traeré	traería
valer *to be worth* valiendo valido	**valgo** vales vale valemos valéis valen	valía	**valdré**	**valdría**
venir *to come* **viniendo** venido	**vengo** **vienes** **viene** venimos venís **vienen**	venía	**vendré**	**vendría**
ver *to see* viendo **visto**	**veo** ves ve vemos veis ven	**veía**	veré	vería

preterite	present subjunctive	imperfect subjunctive	imperative
salí	**salga**	saliera/saliese	
saliste	**salgas**		**sai**
salió	**salga**		
salimos	**salgamos**		
salisteis	**salgáis**		salid
salieron	**salgan**		
fui	**sea**	**fuera/fuese**	
fuiste	**seas**		**sé**
fue	**sea**		
fuimos	**seamos**		
fuisteis	**seáis**		sed
fueron	**sean**		
tuve	**tenga**	**tuviera/tuviese**	
tuviste	**tengas**		**ten**
tuvo	**tenga**		
tuvimos	**tengamos**		
tuvisteis	**tengáis**		tened
tuvieron	**tengan**		
traje	**traiga**	**trajera/trajese**	
trajiste	**traigas**		trae
trajo	**traiga**		
trajimos	**traigamos**		
trajisteis	**traigáis**		traed
trajeron	**traigan**		
valí	**valga**	valiera/valiese	
valiste	**valgas**		vale/**val**
valió	**valga**		
valimos	**valgamos**		
valisteis	**valgáis**		valed
valieron	**valgan**		
vine	**venga**	**viniera/viniese**	
viniste	**vengas**		**ven**
vino	**venga**		
vinimos	**vengamos**		
vinisteis	**vengáis**		venid
vinieron	**vengan**		
vi	**vea**	viera/viese	
viste	**veas**		ve
vio	**vea**		
vimos	**veamos**		
visteis	**veáis**		ved
vieron	**vean**		

▼▼▼ ANSWERS TO ACTIVITIES

▼ *Nouns*
Activity 1
Delante de la estación hay unas **flores** y unos **árboles**; detrás hay dos **trenes** y varios **vagones**. En la calle hay muchos **coches**, cuatro **taxis** y tres **autobuses**. A la derecha hay un almacén que vende **sofás, sillas** y **sillones**.

Activity 2
Estoy pasando **un** día en **un** hotel en **el** centro de **la** cuidad. Desde **el** balcón puedo ver **la** plaza mayor, que tiene **una** fuente grande y **unas** palmeras. A **un** lado está la catedral y **al** otro lado hay **un** parque donde **la** gente está tomando **el** sol. **Al** fondo, **al** pie de **las** montañas y detrás de **la** universidad, se puede ver **el** aeropuerto. Puedo ver **un** avión aterrizar. En **el** cielo hay **unas** nubes.

▼ *Adjectives*
Activity 1
En el **primer** almacén que visitaron los turistas **japoneses** compraron una camisa **azul**, unos calcetines **rojo oscuro**, unos zapatos **marrones**, una chaqueta **gris**, dos camisetas **blancas** y una **gran** toalla **verde**.

Activity 2
a ¿Qué niños son **los más altos**?
Los niños de su hermano son **más altos que** los de su primo, pero los tuyos son **los más altos**.
b ¿Qué fruta es **la menos cara**?
Los plátanos son **menos caros que** las naranjas, pero las manzanas son **las menos caras**.
c ¿Qué platos prefieres?
Los platos azules son **mejores que** los rojos, pero **los peores** son los amarillos.

Activity 3
a ¿De quién son estas cosas?
Los lápices son **míos**, la tinta es **tuya** y las plumas son **de ella**.
b ¿Habéis terminado **vuestro** trabajo?
Nosotros hemos terminado **nuestros** ejercicios, pero él no ha escrito **su** composición todavía
c ¿Son **suyas** (*or* **de Vds.**) estas maletas?
Las maletas verdes son **nuestras** y la pequeña es **mía**, pero las azules allí son **de ellos** y las rojas son **de ellas**.
d ¿Cuál es **tu** bicicleta?
Esta es **mi** bicicleta. La otra es **de él**.

Activity 4
¿Qué has comprado?
He comprado **estas** postales y **este** helado.
Y tú, ¿qué has comprado?
Yo he comprado **estas** castañuelas y **esta** mantilla.

▼ *Adverbs*
Activity 1
finalmente, perfectamente, exactamente, ferozmente, tristemente.

Activity 2
a   Pedro está **locamente** enamorado de Patricia.
b   El guía lo tradujo **bastante** bien.
c   El conductor fue **gravemente** herido en el accidente.
d   **Normalmente** se levanta a las siete.
e   El cumpleaños de su abuelo es hoy **mismo**.

Activity 3
a   Yo no necesito gafas. Puedo ver **mejor** que tú.
b   Le daré el libro a mi sobrino porque le interesa **más** que a mi sobrina.
c   Pepa ganó el premio porque recitó el poema **lo mejor**.
d   ¡Toca la guitarra **menos** alto, Manolo! Estás haciendo demasiado ruido.
e   Andrés nada mal, pero Felipe nada **lo peor** de la clase.

Activity 4
a   Vd. ha gastado **más de** 10.000 pesetas.
b   Está **tan** cansado **que** no puede correr más.
c   La cocina estaba **bastante** limpia.
d   María no parece **tan** enferma **como** Isabel.
e   Ella no tiene **tantos** caballos **como** su amiga.
f   **Cuanto más** trabajaba, **tanto más** se cansaba.
g   El bebé duerme **cada vez menos** ahora.
h   ¿Vd. tiene **bastante** dinero **para** comprar los billetes?
i   Llueve **más** en el sur **que** en el norte.
j   Eduardo no juega al fútbol **tanto como** antes.

▼ *Pronouns*
Activity 1
a   Ustedes **la** vieron.
b   ¡Prepáre**nosla**!
c   El jefe ¿cuándo **se lo** explicó **a él**?
d   María está mostrándo**selos a ellos**. *or* María **se los** está mostrando **a ellos**.
e   ¡No **se los** des **a él**!
f   Ella va a escribír**melo**. *or* Ella **me lo** va a escribir.
g   Nosotros no **nos las** lavamos.
h   José **te la** tradujo.

i **Os los** ha comprado.
j **Lo** puedo devolver mañana. *or* Puedo devolver**lo** mañana.

Activity 2

a El avión en **que** viajó a Nueva York llegó tarde.
b Busco los lápices **que** te presté.
c El director a **quien/que** llamaste no está en la oficina.
d No entendieron todo **lo que** les dijo.
e El profesor **cuyos** estudiantes están allí enseña geografía.
f ¿Qué tazas rompiste? **Las que** estaban cerca de la ventana.
g Trajo sus niñas y **las de** su hermana.
h Conozco los jóvenes con **que/quienes** fuiste a París.
i El río por **el cual** estaba nadando es muy sucio.
j ¿Sabéis **lo que** han escrito en su carta?

Activity 3

a He encontrado **las mías** pero no **las tuyas**.
b Nosotros hemos terminado **los nuestros** pero ellos no han terminado **los suyo/los de ellos**.
c **El mío** pesa más que **el de ella/el suyo**.
d Sí, ha reservado **la vuestra** y **la de ellos** también.
e Me gustaron más **los de ella** que **los de él**.

Activity 4

a ¿Qué sillas te gustan?
Estas son más cómodas que **ésas**, pero las que me gustan más son **aquéllas**.
b ¿Qué piensas de estas novelas?
Esta es más interesante que **ésa**, pero **aquélla** es muy aburrida.
c **Esto** séra muy fácil, pero **eso** será más difícil.

Activity 5

a **Alguien** te ha llamado por teléfono.
b Hay **tanta** gente en la playa hoy.
c ¿Has probado **algunos** de estos licores?
d Parece que **todo el mundo** ha visto esta película.
e Nos estaba contando **algo** muy divertido.
f **Muchas** familias ya tienen su propio ordenador.
g El juguete estaba **del todo** roto.
h Está contenta porque **todo** está en orden.
i **Todo lo** que dice es mentiras.
j El viejecito lee muy **poco** ahora.

▼ *Negatives, Questions, Exclamations*

Activity 1

a **Nadie** estaba mirando la televisión.
b **No** le gusta **ninguna** de estas corbatas.
or **Ninguna** de estas corbatas le gusta.

c **Ni** este coche **ni** el otro es el más caro.
d ¿**No** trabajáis **nunca** en el jardín los fines de semana? *or*
   ¿**Nunca** trabajáis en el jardín los fines de semana?
e **No** han vendido el cuadro **tampoco**. *or*
   Tampoco han vendido el cuadro.

Activity 2
a ¿**Quién** acompañó a tu tía?
b ¿**Cuándo** termina el programa?
c ¿**Qué** secretaria trabaja aquí?
d ¿**De quién** son estos mapas?
e ¿**Cuál** es la calle donde vivieron?
f ¿**Cuál** de estas bebidas prefieren Vds.? *or* ¿**Cuáles** . . . ? *to mean more than one.*
g No sabemos en **qué** hotel pasó la noche.
h Habíamos preguntado a **quiénes** habían invitado.
i Le está explicando **cómo** perdió sus llaves ayer.
j No sabe **cuál/cuáles** escogerá de estas manzanas.

▼ Verbs
Activity 1
a ¿Qué deportes **practicáis** vosotros?
   Yo **nado**, Marta **patina**, y Roberto y Julio **pescan**. Roberto y yo **montamos** a caballo también. Y tú ¿qué deportes **practicas**?

b ¿Qué **bebéis** vosotros generalmente?
   Yo **bebo** cerveza, mis hermanos menores **beben** Coca Cola y mi hermana mayor **bebe** café. Y tú ¿qué **bebes**?

c ¿A quiénes **escribís** vosotros?
   Yo **escribo** a mi hija, Arturo **escribe** a su esposa y ellas **escriben** a su primo. Y tú ¿a quién **escribes**?

Activity 2
a No le **importaba** el precio.
b Nosotros **necesitábamos** el cheque ayer.
c Yo **sabía** lo que **debía** hacer.
d Tú ¿adónde **creías** que ellas **caminaban**?
e Él **aprendía** mucho cada vez que le **enseñaba** ese profesor.
f Ellos **salían** de la oficina a las cinco.

Activity 3
a Los obreros **empezarán** la tarea el jueves.
b Nosotros **atravesaremos** las montañas mañana.
c La criada **subirá** la escalera en seguida.
d Ellos lo **permitirán** sin duda.
e ¿Cuándo me **devolverás** la calculadora, José?
f ¡Ya **veréis** la diferencia, vosotros!

Activity 4
a ¿Qué **tomarías** si tuvieras un dolor de cabeza, Teresa?
  Tomaría una aspirina.
b ¿Cuál **escogeríais** vosotros si tuviérais el dinero?
  Escogeríamos la casa grande con la piscina.
c ¿Adónde **irían** Pablo y Marta si estuvieran libres esta noche?
  Creo que Pablo **iría** a una discoteca y que Marta **visitaría** a su novio.

Activity 5
a ¿Quién **ha jugado** al rugby?
  Nosotros **hemos jugado** al rugby.
b ¿**Has salido** hoy, Conchita?
  No, no **ha salido** nadie.
c ¿**Han subido** los invitados?
  Sí, ya **han subido**.
d ¿**Habéis bebido** la sopa vosotros?
  No, no la **hemos bebido** todavía.

Activity 6
a Ayer **vendí** mi Seat y **compré** un Rover.
b Anoche el Sr. Rodriguez **decidió** ir a Córdoba.
c Los clientes **firmaron** el contrato esta mañana.
d El capitán **encontró** el aeropuerto sin problema.
e Nosotros **comprendimos** en seguida las instrucciones.
f ¿**Mirasteis** en todos los sitios?
g Desafortunadamente **quemaste** el postre.
h ¿Lo **aprendiste** todo, José?
i Vosotros **corristeis** mejor que el otro equipo.

Activity 7
a Nosotros **habíamos escuchado** la radio antes de salir.
b No sabía dónde **habían estado** los prisioneros.
c ¿Preguntaste quién **había vendido** la moto?
d Yo **había terminado** mi libro antes de acostarme.
e No me dijiste que ya **habías corregido** las faltas.

Activity 8
a Creo que ellos ya **habrán comido**.
b **Habrán llegado** los músicos, ¿no?
c Tú **habrás reparado** la máquina antes de mediodía.
d Ella **habrá soñado** en ganar el premio gordo.
e **Habréis aprendido** mucho en ese curso, ¿no, chicos?

Activity 9
a No **habrían tenido** tanto sueño si se hubieran acostado más temprano anoche.
b Suponíamos que el director lo **habría entrevistado** ya.

c Yo te **habría acompañado** si hubiera estado libre.
d Nosotros le **habríamos reconocido** si no hubiera llevado barba.
e Tu mamá esperaba que ya **habrías dado** de comer al perro, María.

Activity 10
a Quiero que Roberto le **pregunte** otra vez.
b Su marido será feliz dondequiera que le **mande** su compañía.
c Era una lástima que Paco no **hubiera encontrado** su reloj.
d Mientras mi hermano **se quedó** en Madrid, visitó muchos museos.
e Dámelo cuando **pases** por aquí, Teresa.
f Cuando **vivía** en el Medio Oriente se quejaba del calor.
g No creía que el Sr. Pérez **saliera** mañana.
h Dudo que Marcos **se haya aburrido**.
i El pintor no se descansará hasta que **termine** su obra.
j Hubiera preferido que vosotros **jugarais** el sábado.
k Aunque Gloria **habla** corrientemente el castellano, no es española.
h **Grite** lo que **grite**, no le oirán a causa del ruido en la calle.
i Dejó las fotos para que nosotros las **miráramos**.
j El tren llegó a tiempo a pesar de que **había nevado** bastante durante la noche.

Activity 11
a Si **olvidas** de ir al banco, avísame.
b Te lo hubiera dicho si tú **hubieras estado** aquí ayer.
c Si **pensaba** que iba a llover, llevaba su impermeable.
d ¿Hubiérais venido si **os hubiérais sentido** mejor?
e Si Vd. **enviara** la carta hoy, llegaría a Roma el lunes o martes.
f Hubiéramos comprado un coche más grande si **hubiéramos tenido** más dinero.
g Si **recibe** una cuenta, la paga inmediatamente.
h Si la Srta. Rodriguez no le **ha llamado**, es porque todavía no ha terminado la conferencia.
i Me preguntaron si nosotros **habíamos probado** la cocina regional cuando estuvimos en Galicia.

Activity 12
a Dardo, ¡**pásame** el azúcar, por favor!
b ¡**Suban** Vds. ahora!
c ¡**Véndaselo**, señorita!
d ¡No **llores** tanto, Juana!
e ¡**Despertaos**, Felipe y Pedro!
f ¡**Casémonos** en octubre!
g ¡No **lo meta** aquí, por favor, señor!
h ¡**Créeme**, Miguel!
i ¡No **pisen** aquí, por favor, señores!
j ¡No **la cambiemos** todavía!
k ¡No **esquiéis** allí, jóvenes! Es peligroso.
l ¡No **lo permitas**, Tomás!

Activity 13

a ¿Qué **estás pensando** ahora, Carlos?
   Yo **estoy pensando** que debo lavar el coche esta tarde.
b ¿Qué **estaban dibujando** Vds. cuando entré?
   Nosotros **estábamos dibujando** un gato.
c ¿Qué **estaréis haciendo** vosotros mañana por la mañana mientras estamos en
   la oficina?
   Mónica **estará jugando** al tenis con su amiga y yo **estaré pintando** el
   comedor.
d ¿Qué **estaba describiendo** Vd. hace unos minutos?
   Yo **estaba describiendo** el hotel donde estuve ayer.

Activity 14

a ¿A qué hora **te levantas** cada día, Pedro?
b Nosotros **nos llamamos** Arturo y Ernesto.
c ¿Qué hicisteis después de **sentaros**?
d Yo no **me perderé** mañana porque tengo mi mapa.
e Nicolás **se rompió** el brazo la semana pasada.
f Ellos no **se aburrieron** anoche.
g Vosotros siempre **os quejabais** de la comida cuando estábamos de vacaciones.
h Estábamos sonriendo para **nosotros** mientras hablaba.
i ¿Estabas leyendo para **ti** cuando sonó el teléfono?
j Podemos vestirnos **a nosotros mismos** ahora, ya que nos sentimos mucho
   mejor.

Activity 15

a Las próximas casas **serán construidas** de madera.
b Los ministros **fueron asesinados** en Granada el mes pasado.
c La frase **fue añadida** antes por el gerente cuando revisó el documento.
d Su pelo **será cortado** mañana por Luisa.
e **Construirán** (*or* **se construirán**) las próximas casas de madera.
f **Asesinaron a** los ministros en Granada el mes pasado.
g **El gerente añadió** la frase antes cuando revisó el documento.
h **Luisa le cortará el** pelo mañana.

▼ *Common structures based on verbs*
Activity 1

Era invierno. **Era** el tres de enero. **Era** de noche cuando Pablo regresó a su casa,
que **estaba** en las afueras de la ciudad. Su casa **era** bastante grande y **estaba**
rodeada de un jardín. **Estaba** muy cansado y no **estaba** muy contento. **Estaba**
pensando en algunas cosas que habían ocurrido durante su día en la oficina.
Estaba para sacar las llaves de su casa cuando oyó un ruido raro. No sabía lo que
era. El cielo **estaba** muy oscuro. Las luces de su casa **estaban** apagadas y no
podía ver casi nada. Su mujer no **estaba** en la casa porque **estaba** de vacaciones
con una amiga. Pablo **estaba** muy asustado. **Estaba** seguro que había un ladrón
en el jardín. Miró entorno suyo y vio lo que **era**. Llegó a **ser** nada más que el
perro enorme de su vecino.

Activity 2
- ¿**Puedes** ir al baile esta noche, Ana?
- **Tal vez**. ¿Cuándo **hay que** llegar? No, tengo muchas cosas que **debo** hacer. **Tengo que** terminar una carta a mi tía, pero también **debería** ayudar a mi mamá en la cocina. Mis padres han invitado a unos amigos a cenar. El problema es que **no sé** cocinar muy bien. ¿Me **podrías** ayudar?
- No estoy segura. **Hubiera podido** ayudaros esta mañana porque estaba libre. Pero esta tarde **he debido** prometer a mi mamá que haría unas compras para ella y que arreglaría mi cuarto. ¿Te ha llamado, Isabel?
- No, **debe de haber** olvidado.

Activity 3
a ¿A tus hermanos **les encanta** volar?
  A ella **le encanta** volar, pero a él no.
b ¿Cuántos sellos **les faltan** a Vds.?
  Nos faltan cuatro.
c ¿Qué **te hace falta** hacer todavía en la oficina, Victoria?
  Me hace falta enviar un fax a una compañía en Buenos Aires.
d ¿Cuánta gasolina **nos queda** a nosotros?
  Nos quedan 15 litros.
e ¿Dónde **le duele**, señorita?
  Me duele aquí en la cabeza.
f ¿Qué **os interesa** más, jóvenes, los programas deportivos o los documentales?
  Nos interesan más los programas deportivos.

Activity 4
a ¿Desde cuándo **vives** en Inglaterra, Carmen?
  Vivo en Inglaterra **desde hace** diez años.
  or **Hace** diez años **que** vivo en Inglaterra.
b ¿Cuánto tiempo hace que **se marcharon**?
  Hace cinco días **que** se marcharon.
  or Se marcharon **desde hace** cinco días.
c ¿Desde cuándo creía que no **había llovido**?
  Creía que no había llovido **desde** agosto.
d ¿Cuánto tiempo **llevan** Vds. **trabajando** en ventas?
  Llevamos ocho meses **trabajando** en ventas.
  or **Hace** ocho meses **que** trabajamos en ventas.
  or Trabajamos en ventas **desde hace** ocho meses.
e ¿Desde cuándo **habían sido** colonizadas las islas cuando ganaron su independencia?
  Las islas habían sido colonizadas **desde hace** tres siglos cuando ganaron su independencia.
f ¿Hacía cuánto tiempo dijo que ella **estudiaba** en la universidad?
  Dijo que ella estudiaba en la universidad **desde hacía** dos años y medio.

▼▼▼
INDEX